Business Strategy

Essentials You Always Wanted To Know

CW00968349

- Scanning
- Value Chain
- Purpose
- Strategy Level
- Five Level
- Monitoring
- External Analysis
- Environmental Scanning
- Formulation
- Competitive Dynamics
- Forecasting
- Assessing
- Business Strategy
- Rivalry
- Cross Boarder
- Mergers & Acquisition
- Horizontal Growth
- Barriers
- New Capabilities
- Reforming Scope
- Execution
- Vertical Growth
- Strategic Change
- Culture
- Leadership

VIBRANT
PUBLISHERS

Business
Strategy
Essentials You Always Wanted To Know

© 2019, By Vibrant Publishers, USA. All rights reserved. No part of this publication may be reproduced or distributed in any form or by any means, or stored in a database or retrieval system, without the prior permission of the publisher.

ISBN-10: 1-946383-98-8
ISBN-13: 978-1-946383-98-3
Library of Congress Control Number: 2018905413

This publication is designed to provide accurate and authoritative information in regard to the subject matter covered. The Author has made every effort in the preparation of this book to ensure the accuracy of the information. However, information in this book is sold without warranty either expressed or implied. The Author or the Publisher will not be liable for any damages caused or alleged to be caused either directly or indirectly by this book.

The publisher wishes to thank Kalpesh Ashar (India) for his valuable inputs to this edition

Vibrant Publishers books are available at special quantity discount for sales promotions, or for use in corporate training programs. For more information please write to **bulkorders@vibrantpublishers.com**

Please email feedback / corrections (technical, grammatical or spelling) to **spellerrors@vibrantpublishers.com**

To access the complete catalogue of Vibrant Publishers, visit
www.vibrantpublishers.com

Table of Contents

Chapter **1** Introduction to Business Strategy   9

Definition and Features   9
Strategic Statement   10
Strategic Management Influences   12
Who's Who of Strategic Management   14

Chapter **2** Understanding Industry   17

Industry Life Cycle   18
Industry Structure (Porter's Five Forces)   21
Case Study   29

Chapter **3** Processes and Phases in Strategy Management   33

Environmental Scanning   35
Case Study   50

Chapter **4** External Analysis   51

Environments – General   52
Environments – Competitive   59
Case Study   61

Chapter **5** Formulation of Strategy   63

Strategy Levels   63

Chapter **6** Corporate Level Strategy   93

Diversification Levels   94
Creating Value with Diversification   96
Value Neutral Diversification   102
Value Reducing Diversification   104

Chapter **7**   Mergers and Acquisitions   105

     Increasing Market Power   109
     Barriers to Entry   110
     Cross Border Acquisitions   110
     Producing New Goods and Speediness to Market   111
     New Products are Higher Risk   111
     Reforming Scope   112
     New Capabilities   112
     Issues   112
     What Makes an Acquisition Successful?   117
     Restructuring   119
     Case Study   121

Chapter **8**   Execution of Strategy   123

     Structure of Organization   123
     Vertical Growth   125
     Horizontal Growth   126
     Alternative Structural Forms   127
     Evaluating Organizational Structure   131
     Executing Strategic Change   134

Dear Reader,

Thank you for purchasing **Business Strategy Essentials You Always Wanted To Know**. We are committed to publishing books that are content-rich, concise and approachable enabling more readers to read and make the fullest use of them. We hope this book provides you the most enriching learning experience.

This **Self-Learning Management Series** intends to give a jump start to working professionals, whose job roles demand to have the knowledge imparted in a B-school but haven't got a chance to visit one. This series is designed to address every aspect of business from HR to Finance to Marketing to Operations, be it any industry. Each book includes basic fundamentals, important concepts, standard and well-known principles as well as practical ways of application of the subject matter. The distinctiveness of the series lies in that all the relevant information is bundled in a compact form that is very easy to interpret.

Should you have any questions or suggestions, feel free to email us at **reachus@vibrantpublishers.com**

Thanks again for your purchase.

– Vibrant Publishers Team

Self-Learning
Management Series

Cost Accounting and
Management Essentials You
Always Wanted To Know

ISBN: 978-1-946383-62-4

Financial Accounting
Essentials You Always
Wanted To Know

ISBN: 978-1-946383-66-2

Project Management
Essentials You Always
Wanted To Know

ISBN: 978-1-946383-60-0

Financial Management
Essentials You Always
Wanted To Know

ISBN: 978-1-946383-64-8

Principles of Management
Essentials You Always
Wanted To Know

ISBN: 978-1-946383-93-8

Business Strategy
Essentials You Always
Wanted To Know

ISBN: 978-1-946383-98-3

Marketing Management
Essentials You Always
Wanted To Know

ISBN: 978-1-949395-04-4

For the most updated list of books visit
www.vibrantpublishers.com

facebook.com/vibrantpublishers

Preface

Being tasked with developing a vision of the future of your organization and the steps to ensure that successful vision is a daunting task that many organizations fail at. Organizations fail to do an adequate industry or competitive analysis. Their environmental scanning is not thorough, or they don't act on what they found. Their strategies may be inappropriate for their industry and current industry position. High level management does not buy into the strategies and support it, or employees are not bought in. These are just a few of the examples of common mistakes made that can cause organizations to fail in their industries and ultimately go out of business. So, how do you in successfully implementing strategy when there are so many that have failed that have gone before you?

Business Strategy Essentials You Always Wanted To Know seeks to guide you in answering this question. This book consists of core elements of strategy that have been learned from past failures and successes. Working with strategies, you may be faced with challenges such as developing a strategic statement, developing an industry analysis, dealing with aggressive competitor moves, and communicating strategy to employees. These items are included in this book along with several other elements to help anyone understand and function in their role of managing strategy. Using real life experiences and detailed study, this handbook will give you the tools to get started.

This page is intentionally left blank

Chapter **1**

Introduction to Business Strategy

Why is strategic management needed in the business place? Businesses want to be successful and in order to that, they must be able to make intelligent decisions. How do you know what the intelligent decision is and what decision to make? That is where strategic management comes into play. Strategic management guides the organization's future growth using effective and efficient management methods with an emphasis on setting appropriate goals.

Definition and Features

Strategic management consists of decisions around corporate finances, human resources, mission, vision, and values, etc. These decisions cannot be made in a vacuum. Organizations that are most effective in their strategic management have great communication, effective management and leadership. This structure of organizational governance is critical because, without it, you do not have the organizational buy-in needed to effectively set goals and make decisions. Organizational governance is also used to control and report on how we are performing to the strategic goals we have set.

Strategic management is also a great way to pinpoint what your organization's core competencies and get the most out of them. Core competencies are difficult for a competitor to recreate, provides value to the consumer, and it can be utilized in various products and/or services. Examples of core competencies may simply be the name of the brand or the cost of production. Really understanding what those core competencies are for your organization will allow you to know what causes your organization's success.

A well-defined strategy can be an excellent roadmap for your organization. Not only does the strategy detail the organization mission, vision, and values, it demonstrates to others where the organization wants to be in the future. It is important to have a thorough strategy in order to plan for different situations in the future since nothing is finite. The strategy focuses mainly on long term advances rather than short term progress. Strategy also works to consider the behaviors of consumers, competitors, and employees in its planning.

Strategic Statement

During formulation, the organization focuses on a statement of their strategy. This statement includes the following elements:

strategic intent, mission, vision, and objectives. An organization's strategy statement shapes the organization's long-term strategic path and overall policy directions. With this statement, the organization can outline their map for long term activities.

Strategic intent is part of the strategy statement. This is the reason that the organization is in place today and why it will continue to function in years to come. The strategic intent gives the big picture about an organization that motivates and inspires employees. Priorities are clarified and a clear direction to assist in setting goals and influence resources and core competencies.

Another piece of the strategy statement is the mission statement. The mission statement is formulated to detail how the organization expects to serve its stakeholders. It gives the "why", "what" and "who" behind an organization. Why is this organization in existence? What does it do or produce? Who does it serve? Mission statements are created to set apart one organization from another. For example, you could say that Wal-Mart and Target are similar stores and therefore have similar answers to the questions above. However, the heart behind what they do and why they do it are completely different. A good mission statement is achievable, clearly stated, motivating, precise, original, investigative, and credible.

Vision is also a critical component. This statement is different from the mission statement in that it focuses on where the organization plans to be in the future. Essentially, the vision statement is what the organization wants to be when it grows up. The mission statement go hand in hand. The vision statement describes what the organization will be like if it is successful in achieving its mission. A good vision statement is explicit, clear, in line with organization's cultures and values, realistic, and less lengthy than the mission statement so it can be memorized.

The final component of the strategic statement includes the objectives and goals. A goal is something that an organization is trying to achieve. An objective is a goal we wish to reach over a specified period of time. Goals and objectives break down the mission and vision into more digestible elements. Goals are what we want to reach in order to achieve our mission and vision. Ideal goals and objectives should be exact and measurable, realistic, have defined time frames, address significant issues, and include both financial and non-financial components. Objectives help us to plan how we will meet our goals. Organizations typically have several objectives that can be long term or short term. Objectives are more agile and can change to the environment. Finally, objectives are realistic and operational.

Strategic Management Influences

The discipline of strategic management has been around since the 1950s and was referred to as "business policy". Today, this field pulls from several different perspectives and studies to make up its content. At its core, its roots can be traced to three main theories.

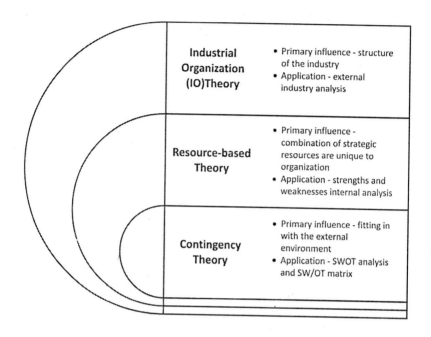

Industrial Organization (IO)Theory	• Primary influence - structure of the industry • Application - external industry analysis
Resource-based Theory	• Primary influence - combination of strategic resources are unique to organization • Application - strengths and weaknesses internal analysis
Contingency Theory	• Primary influence - fitting in with the external environment • Application - SWOT analysis and SW/OT matrix

Industrial organization theory focuses on how the industry environment can affect an organization. This theory says that, in order for an organization to survive and thrive, they must be agile with the changes in the industry. To take it a step further, if the industry is thriving, this theory says that the organization will be thriving.IO states that organization success is heavily dependent upon how easily it can change to meet the industry forces. Therefore, in order to have a successful strategy, the organization must have a good understanding of the nature of the industry and how it changes so it can develop strategies that coincide with the industry's movements. You can see IO playing out in industries when a competitor implements a new piece of functionality, technology, or product. The other competitors in the industry will quickly work to replicate that new item. For example, when Apple introduces a new piece of functionality in their iPhone, competitors like Samsung will quickly work to replicate that functionality on their phones and vice versa.

Resource-based theory says that an organization is only as good as how well they use their resources. This theory states that an organization can be successful if it can effectively and efficiently utilize the resources they have at hand. This ability gives the organization a competitive advantage. This theory indicates that the resources of an organization are closely linked with its competencies which, in turn, create worth and lead to financial success. This theory looks mainly at individual organizations and less at the industry environment as a whole.

Contingency theory, in a sense, takes both of the theories above into account. It states that an organization is successful when they make decisions led by their mission, the competitive environment, and use of its resources. Contingency theory says the performance of an organization is a result of the industry forces and the organization's individual strategic actions. In order to be successful, organizations should have strengths and weaknesses that coincide with the industry's opportunities and threats. This theory even goes so far as to say that if there is a dramatic change in the industry that is detrimental to the organization, consideration should be given to pulling out of the industry all together and moving to another industry.

Who's Who of Strategic Management

Implementing strategies is more complicated than top management simply telling other leaders to reach specific goals and objectives. There is a governance structure involved to ensure proper development and implementation of strategies. When we refer to corporate governance, we are referencing board of directors, investors, shareholders, etc. An organization's board of directors' monitors undertakings in the organization, assesses strategies proposed by leaders, and sets the overall strategic path. The board of directors must take into account the viewpoints of the major shareholders in the organization when making decisions and approving strategies. After the board of directors approves the final strategy, they look to the top leadership of the organization (chief officers) to make the strategy happen. Chief Officers work with top managers to break down the strategies into organizational goals. Top managers collaborate with midlevel and front-line managers to break down the organizational goals built from the strategies even further into individual departments' objectives.

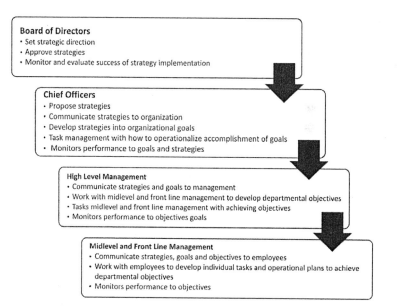

This page is intentionally left blank

Chapter **2**

Understanding Industry

Before diving into the processes and phases behind strategic management, it is important to understand industry and industry competition because this external analysis is a vital part of strategic planning. First, industry is described as a group of businesses that provide competing goods or services. Each industry is unique in its products, pricing, distribution, and quality requirements. They have developed their own "normal". For example, in the healthcare industry, a medical practice usually provides outpatient services to its patients, sometimes provide medications, and may even provide medical equipment. Medical practices in the industry abide by these norms in order to compete effectively in the industry. If some medical practices decided that it was also going to sell cars, they would be going outside the norms of the industry and possibly jeopardizing their ability to be successful. It is possible to step outside of the industry normal and add new products and services but when organizations deviate too far, they typically fail. Due to this, managers tasked with developing strategic plans should be very knowledgeable of the industry they work in, so they can develop plans that help them to compete successfully.

Once an organization has defined the industry it competes in, they should examine the market share of the industry players. Market share is how much of the total industry sales is contributed to by a specific competitor. If market share is unavailable, relative market share can be analyzed. Relative market share is an organization's portion of industry sales when you only take into account the organization itself and its key competitors. Looking at either of these, gives the organization an idea of where they stand in the industry today, so they can determine where they want to be in the long term. After determining this, strategies can begin to be developed to reach the goal end state.

Industry Life Cycle

Industries are dynamic, they change over time. In order to be most successful in planning, managers need to understand the life cycle of industries to plan accordingly.

Introduction	Growth	Shakeout	Maturity	Decline
• Low demand • First time buyers	• Rising demand • Market approaches saturation	• Growth slows • Small group of industry leaders	• Very little new buyers • Standards for quality and service established	• Demand decreases • Substitute industries grow in popularity

The introduction phase is characterized by its low demand. Practically all buyers are first time buyers. The industry is in its infancy and demand for outputs is low. Consumers are just becoming aware. This is a stage that organizations typically go through quickly. They rely on technology to help the create efficiencies in production. Buyers heavily scrutinize the product offered which could may cause some organizations to fail in the industry. Organizations that survive the scrutiny with a legitimate solution move on to the next phase.

The growth phase is not exactly as it sounds. Although growth does continue, it begins to slow due to market saturation. Efficiencies gained with technology begin to be perfected and any issues with the technology itself is resolved. The number of first time buyers dwindles. Buyers are now purchasing product upgrades, replacements, or add-ons. Many competitors in the industry begin to see a profit but they are taking that profit and investing it in research and development in an attempt to get ahead of the curve on newer technologies and advancements in the product. Organizations that are weaker may decide to leave the industry because they cannot compete.

The shakeout phase is characterized by a market saturation of competitors that causes a slowdown in growth due to inability of the industry to support the number of competitors. At this phase, core competencies really come into play to set you apart from the other competitors since expanding your growth is not as feasible. The main players in the industry surface while competitors on the fringe phase out.

During maturity, growth virtually grinds to a halt or even goes into a negative direction. For the most part, buyers are only purchasing upgrades and replacements. Quality and services standards have been determined and the expectations of the consumer aren't in flux as they had been in previous stages. Organizations begin to look at other ways their products or services can be used so they can open up new opportunities and enter new markets. This growth may be as simple as expanding from a national industry to a global industry.

The final stage of decline happens when consumer demand decreases, and they began to look to other sources for more convenient and costly solutions. An example of this would be the decline of the typewriter industry due to growth of computers. Consumers began to purchase computers in lieu of typewriters because they got more value for their money. At this point, companies either dissociate from the industry or they look to recreate themselves with a new product or service. Kodak was very popular in the 1980's and 1990's for their cameras. They were one of the top competitors in the market. As the digital camera began to make its appearance on the market, the demand for Kodak's non-digital cameras declined. They were unable to keep up with the speed of the developing technology in the digital camera market and ultimately went out of business.

Understanding the stage of the life cycle the industry is in is important, however, organizations cautioned not to put too much emphasis on the stage when strategically planning. There are several reasons for this. First, external forces can accelerate or decelerate the movement of the industry through the cycle. External forces are unable to be controlled and sometimes unpredictable. Also, some industries do not follow this life cycle exactly. They may jump over a stage to another phase. Predicting the pace at which the industry will go through the phases is also a great challenge. Finally, hyper competition can cause issues if heavily relied on in planning. Hyper competition is the idea that industries appear, develop, and change so quickly that some organizations can find it difficult to stay in the current stage or staying in the current stage becomes a task that is not worthwhile.

Industry Structure (Porter's Five Forces)

Industry structure is described as the size and number of competitors in the industry. There are factors that correlate with industry structure that can affect whether an organization does well or fails. These factors are:

a) Level of intensity of competition between organizations

b) Level of threat that a new organization will enter the industry

c) Level of threat that another product or service can be substituted

d) How much bargaining power the buyer yields

e) How much bargaining power the supplier yields

These five factors make up the industry structure factors that affect profitability for organizations. They are often referred to as Porter's Five Forces Model of Competition. Let's look at each of these factors at a more in-depth level.

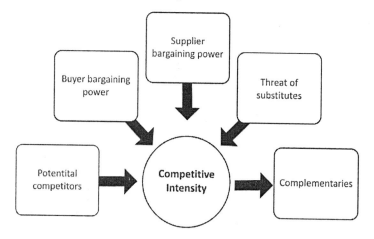

Competitive Intensity

Intensity of competition between competitors in an industry is the level that organizations put pressure on each other and try to minimize their profit potential. If the level is high, competitors aggressively aim at one another's markets and engage in price wars on products. Advertising battles can ensue as well. When the intensity level is high, the profitability potential for an organization is reduced. The opposite is also true. When the intensity level is low, the profitability potential is increased. If there are a large number of competitors in the industry, the intensity level is likely to be high. If the market share or competitors are equal size, then competition is increased. If the growth of the industry itself is slow, competition is increased. If the fixed costs in the industry are high, the intensity is also increased. Other reasons that intensity would be high are if brand loyalty is low, competitors are diverse, production capacity is high, and if the cost of exiting the industry is high.

The wireless phone services industry is an excellent example of a high level of competitive intensity. Verizon and Sprint are at constant battle with each other with their advertising blatantly voicing the disadvantages of the competitors. When one firm advertises a wireless package for a low rate, the other quickly tries to match that rate. This has most recently happened with free data becoming available in packages. After Sprint released their offering of free data with their wireless package, Verizon also offered free data with their packages as well.

Another highly competitive industry is the airline industry. The cost of fares is no longer based on the airline's cost to fly you from one place to another. It is highly influenced by competitive pressures from airlines that fly more limited places for a lower rate. The organizations that were typically the top players in the industry, flying everywhere are having to reduce their rates to match the smaller competitors. This, in turn, is affecting their profitability.

Competitive intensity decreases if the opposite is true of all of the high intensity characteristics mentioned above.

a) Few organizations in the industry

b) Market leader is clear

c) Industry grows rapidly

d) Fixed costs are low

e) Product differentiation is high

f) Clear brand loyalties

g) Cost of a consumer to switch is high

h) Production capacity is low

i) Little strategic diversity

j) Exit costs are low

Threat of New Entrants

What level of threat do new competitors present to existing organizations in the industry? This is the question we ask when we are considering the threat of entry of new competitors. If it is easy for new competitors to enter the market, the threat to existing organizations is high. Increased production capacity without an increase in consumer demand translates to less profit for organizations. New competitors can affect market share, product quality, and price levels detrimentally. If there is a high threat, the industry can become more competitive and decrease potential profit with organizations existing in the industry. The reverse is also true. A low threat can reduce competitiveness of an industry and increase potential profit. To reduce the threat of new organizations entering the industry, barriers to entry into the industry must increase.

Increased economies of scale can increase the barriers to entry. This means that the costs savings gained by an increased level of production is disproportionate. Industry leaders that have highly specialized products or high brand loyalty can increase the barriers to entry as well. Another barrier is large upfront capital investments needed to enter into the industry. When the switching costs for consumers is high, the threat of a new organization entering the market is low. Other barriers include impeded access to desired locations and patented technology or production material inputs.

Again, the reverse of all of the items listed above will decrease barriers and result in a high level of threat of entry of new organizations. These include:

a) No economies of scale

b) Standardized products

c) Low upfront capital investment

d) Consumer switching costs are low

e) Distribution channels are easily accessible

f) No advantage to a specific locale

g) No advantage to proprietary assets

Another factor that can affect entry into an industry is governmental regulations and policies. For some industries, the government actually polices the number of new entrants and existing organizations using regulations and licensing requirements. A great example of this would be the creation of a new hospital, skilled nursing facility, or outpatient surgery center. The government requires certain licensing and approval to build any of these facilities.

Substitute Products

When a product is available that a buyer can purchase instead of the industry's product, there is a threat of a substitute product. Substitute products are from another industry and they offer comparable advantages to the industry's offering. If a consumer buys a substitute product, they are influencing the organizations as well as the industry's ability to profitable. This can also cause the industry to become more competitive and there for reduce the potential for profit. The inverse is also true. If there are not any close substitute products, the industry becomes less competitive and more profitable.

There is a high-level threat from substitute products when:

a) Low consumer costs for switching

b) Substitute product costs the consumer less

c) Substitute product is equal or higher quality

d) Substitute product's utilities, qualities, or performance are equal or higher quality

When any of these items are occurring, profitability in the industry reduces as well as profitability at the individual organization. Consumers have switched their buying to another industry all together, so the alternative industry and organization are seeing the profits.

As with the other threats, the opposite is also true. There is a low-level threat from substitute products when:

a) Consumer costs for switching are high

b) Substitute product costs the consumer more

c) Substitute product is lesser quality

d) Substitute product's utilities, qualities, or performance are lesser quality

When this is occurring in an industry, profits can remain with the individual organizations and inside the industry because consumers are not buying the alternative.

Buyer Bargaining Power

The bargaining power of a buyer refers to the influence consumers have on businesses to require them to provide higher quality solutions, better customer service, and lower prices. Buyers exert this influence by playing one organization against the other. The competitive environment and profitability in the industry is affected by the power of buyer bargaining. Sellers are pressured to reduce prices, increase quality, and offer more and improved services. To meet these demands, there are costs to the seller. Therefore, if the buyer is strong, they can reduce the potential profit for the seller and increase competition in the industry. If the buyer is weak, the opposite is true. The industry competition reduces and profit potential increases.

What factors determine the buyer's bargaining power? First, if there are more sellers than buyers, the buyer has the upper hand and therefore the bargaining power. If the switching costs for a buyer are low, the buyer has more bargaining power. If the consumer can somehow make the product themselves, their bargaining power is increased. Other factors affecting bargaining power include buyer price sensitivity, product education, large volume purchases, and substitute products can be purchased.

On the other hand, the opposite of these items reduces the buyer's bargaining power. So, the buyer's bargaining power is low when:

a) More buyers than sellers

b) Switching costs are high

c) Buyers cannot produce the product themselves

d) Little price sensitivity

e) Buyers are uneducated

f) Consumers buy specialized products

g) No substitute products

Supplier Bargaining Power

Supplier bargaining power is described as the influence suppliers have on organizations by affecting prices, quality, and availability of their products. Using these actions, suppliers can affect the competitiveness of the industry and the organization's profitability. Suppliers that are stronger can push organizations by increasing prices, reducing quality of the product, and limiting availability of the product. All of these actions result in costs to the organizations. With these actions, the supplier also affects the industry itself by making it more competitive and reducing the potential for profit for the organizations. If you look at the opposite, if a supplier is weak, they are reliant on the organizations to determine quality and price, so the industry becomes less competitive and the profit potential for the organizations increase.

Bargaining power for sellers is high when there are more buyers than sellers. If the cost of switching from one supplier to another is high, seller bargaining power is also increased. If the supplier can produce the buyer's product themselves, the power to bargain is greater. If price sensitivity and increased knowledge of the products are not a buyer issue, suppliers have more power. If there is high product differentiation, a large part of suppliers' sales are not buyers, and substitute products are not available, the supplier's power is increased.

Examining the opposite, the supplier's power is low when:

a) Less buyers than sellers

b) Switching costs are low

c) Cannot produce buyers' product

d) Increased buyer sensitivity

e) Buyers are well-educated

f) Buyers purchase large amounts

g) Substitute products are available.

There are some experts who add a sixth force to Porters' forces. This force is called complementors. Complementors are organizations that offer add-on products or services to the products sold in a specific industry. An example of this would be cases for Apple iPhones. Otterbox produces cases for iPhones which is a complementary product to the iPhone itself. When there are complementors in available, the competitive structure of the industry is highly influenced.

Considerations of Porter's Five Forces

This model is based on the industrial organization theory and has some limitations that should be considered. The first assumption of Porter's Five Forces is that the industry is clearly definable and distinguishable. There are many industries that are growing in complexity which make clearly defining the industry a challenge. Also, the model focuses on individual organizations and does not account for partnerships in industries which is increasingly happening. Porter's Five Forces also does not take into account industries that are highly affected by organizational lobbyists. Lobbyists can work with government to modify the industry structure with different regulations. Organizations in the healthcare industry employ lobbyists specifically for this purpose. Another issue with this model is that is relies on industry factors and not the organization's internal resources to be the main determinants of profitability. Lastly, this model does not account for organizations who are working in multiple countries. In this case, the organization would have to consult many industry structures to glean the information which can become quite complex.

Case Study

Let's understand Porter's Five Forces in a real-life example. Walmart began in the discount store industry as a small single store and is now one of the largest retailers in the worlXd. They are in 28 countries and has a strong internet presence. They have millions of employees worldwide. Walmart's main focus is to provide low prices every day on a wide variety of products anytime or anywhere a customer visits a Walmart store.

If we look closer at Walmart, we can examine where they stand with a five forces analysis.

a) **Intensity of rivalry** – there is a large amount of competitive rivalry between Walmart and Target. The following circumstances exist:

    i. Competitors aggressively aim at one another's markets and engage in price wars on products (high factor)

    ii. Advertising battles.

    iii. Profitability potential for an organization is reduced.

    iv. Large number of competitors in the industry (high factor)

    v. Market share or competitors are equal size

    vi. Slow industry growth

    vii. High fixed costs

  viii. Low brand loyalty

  ix. Diverse competitors

  x. High production capacity

  xi. Exit costs high

b) **Bargaining power of buyers** – low, buyers do not have power to dictate price. The following circumstances exist:

  i. More buyers than sellers (high factor)

  ii. Switching costs are high

  iii. Buyers cannot produce the product themselves

  iv. Little price sensitivity

  v. Buyers are uneducated

  vi. Consumers buy specialized products

  vii. No substitute products

c) **Bargaining power of suppliers** – low, suppliers do not have power to dictate cost. The following circumstances exist:

  i. Less buyers than sellers (high factor)

  ii. Switching costs are low

  iii. Cannot produce buyers' product

  iv. Increased buyer sensitivity

  v. Buyers are well-educated

  vi. Buyers purchase large amounts

d) **Substitute products are available threat of substitutes** – low, the closest thing to a substitute would be a dollar store or dollar general but they do not have the variety or brand names that Walmart has. The following circumstances exist:

  i. Consumer costs for switching are high

  ii. Substitute product costs the consumer more

  iii. Substitute product is lesser quality

iv. Substitute product's utilities, qualities, or performance are lesser quality

e) **Threat of new entrants** – this threat is strong due to the following:

    i. No economies of scale – (high factor)

    ii. Standardized product-s

    iii. Low upfront capital investment – (high factor)

    iv. Consumer switching costs are low

    v. Distribution channels are easily accessible

    vi. No advantage to a specific locale

    vii. No advantage to proprietary assets

The analysis tells us that Walmart needs to be cognizant and have strategies ready for the threat of new entrants and intense competitive rivalry. Long term strategies should focus on maintaining their competitive advantage with focus on new entrants and competitors. As you can see in the competitive rivalry section, Walmart needs to make sure they have a defensive and offensive strategy to act quickly since competitors are aggressive in their markets.

With bargaining power of buyers, there is a high factor of a large population of buyers, however since there are a wide variety of buyers who typically make small purchases, this becomes a low impact issue. It is similar with bargaining power of suppliers. There is a large population of suppliers but, since Walmart stores are so large, they actually compete for small spaces in their stores to sell their products. Also, since there is a high availability out there of the products, they have little impact on Walmart. Substitutes are very available for Walmart's goods. The variety of substitutes for all of the things that Walmart sells is very low and often cost more. Therefore, this force is not a large issue for

Walmart either.

Entering Walmart's market is costly because you have to develop a brand name that can compete with Walmart which can take a substantial amount of time. Consider that Walmart spent 50 years developing their brand. This force works in Walmart's favor. However, the costs of opening a new competitor store and running it are not high which makes Walmart's market very attractive to new entrants.

Chapter 3

Processes and Phases in Strategy Management

The overall backbone of any organization is incorporated in its strategy. Strategic management is formulated by top management and is where all management levels meet with shared goals. Strategic management gives organizations rules, policies, procedures, priorities, and direction for long term success. The entire process of strategic management occurs in four stages that can recur and is also referred to as the Strategic cycle. These four stages are:

a) **Environmental Scanning** – collecting data on external and internal factors and analyzing it to see how it may affect the organization

b) **Formulation** – determining how the organization wants to proceed in consideration of all the information collected. The organization decides what the next steps are in achieving organizational goals and objectives. Business and functional strategies are developed.

c) **Implementation** – putting the decisions made into action. Breaking down the strategy to help determine things such as organizational structure, resourcing, and decision making.

d) **Evaluation** – take into consideration the internal and external factors that drive the strategies that are in place now. Measure how the organization is performing, and course correct.

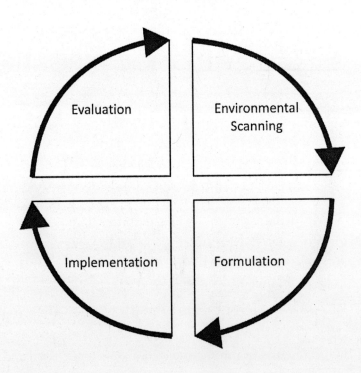

Environmental Scanning

Scanning of the environment is a critical first step in the process of strategic management. It is important to examine what is happening externally and internally in the organization before determining what strategies to implement. Examples of items you would look for externally could include trends in the industry, governmental regulations, patterns, and competitor activities. Internally, you may want to look at things like employee communications and relationships, management interaction and activities, and shareholder activities. This environmental scanning is often completed through a SWOT analysis. (Strengths, Weaknesses, Opportunities, and Threats)

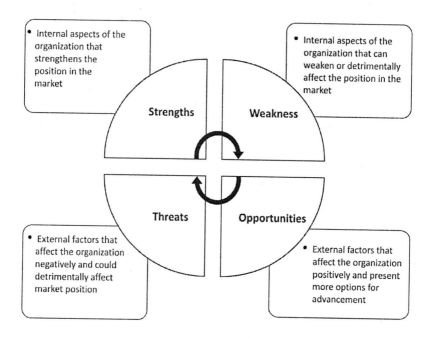

Internal Analysis

Internal analysis of the organizational environment allows you to determine the organization's strengths and weaknesses. By understanding the resources and abilities of your organization, you can identify and capitalize on competitive advantages.

By exploiting the strengths and minimizing exposure of the weaknesses, an organization gains an edge on the competition. The organization has found a way to create value for their consumers. Value is what the consumer is willing to pay for in terms of performance characteristics and attributes. Value is the key to above average returns for an organization. Below is an illustration of how resources, capabilities, core competencies, competitive advantage and strategic competitiveness is interrelated.

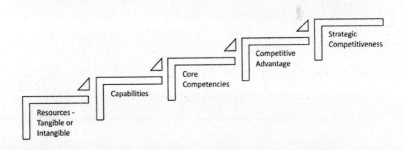

Internal analysis is very challenging for managers because the decisions that have to be made are not routine decisions, must be examined ethically, and affects the organization's profitability potential. Before strategic decisions can be made, managers must know what the organization's core competencies are. At the least, the manager should understand the core competencies that are related to going into or leaving new industries, financing new technologies, adding additional manufacturing capacity, and forming strategic relationships.

The challenge in making strategic decisions is that there is a high risk that the company's plans may fail due to interpretation errors. The upside to this is that bad decisions can be corrected if you act quickly and gather the appropriate information to implement the right corrective action. Making these mistakes, can in a sense, be a competitive advantage itself because organizations learn what not to do.

It is helpful to identify the more challenging strategic decisions that need to be made before implementing a plan. Doing this, allows the organization to be very deliberate in data gathering and information interpretation before developing a strategic plan.

Typically, the more challenging strategic decisions have a level of:

a) **Uncertainty** – unsure of the qualities of the general and/or industry environments, how competitors may act, and what the consumer prefers

b) **Complexity** – causes shaping the environments and viewpoints of the environments are complexly interrelated

c) **Intraorganizational conflicts** – managers making the decisions and who are affected by these decisions are not in agreement

Decision makers make strategic decisions through learning. They determine if the probability of a certain mistake happening is worth the impact. When a mistake is acknowledged, it is adjusted rapidly, and identification of new possibilities and capabilities occur. Good judgment goes hand in hand with good outcomes in strategic planning. Decision makers may choose to take an educated risk based on the gathered information in decision itself, possible outcomes, possible risks and possible impacts. When good judgment is used, strategic competitiveness is accomplished.

Resources

Resource is one of the key components of competitive advantage. When we bundle resources, we can create a competitive advantage. Resources alone do not generate competitive advantage. At the center of an organization's abilities are resources and they are widespread in scope. This scope can include individual, social and organizational resources. Resources contribute to an organization's production process with two types of resources: tangible and intangible.

Tangible resources can be processed by any of the five senses. Examples of tangible resources can be people, money, or computer hardware. The types of tangible resources you find in an organization are financial, organizational, physical, and technological.

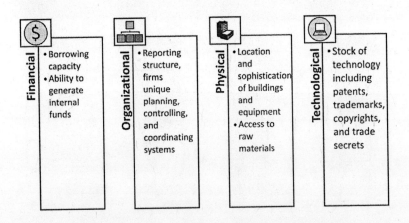

Financial
- Borrowing capacity
- Ability to generate internal funds

Organizational
- Reporting structure, firms unique planning, controlling, and coordinating systems

Physical
- Location and sophistication of buildings and equipment
- Access to raw materials

Technological
- Stock of technology including patents, trademarks, copyrights, and trade secrets

There are some constraints to the tangible resources. When considering that financial resources can be identified from financial statements, we have to remember that the value of all of the organization's assets is not necessarily reflected in a financial statement. The statement does not take into consideration the intangible resources. Another constraint is that it is challenging to leverage these resources because developing additional business or value from a tangible resource is difficult. For example, you can utilize one team in five different places at the same time. It is also important to remember that some of the processes utilized with tangible assets are intangible. Therefore, it is important to look at resources from both a tangible and intangible viewpoint to ensure you have captured all of your resources.

Intangible resources are typically accumulated over time and are a part of the organization's history. These resources cannot be seen or touched. Examples of intangible resources are knowledge, capabilities of management, trust between leadership and employees, and reputation. There are three types of intangible resources: human, innovation, and reputational.

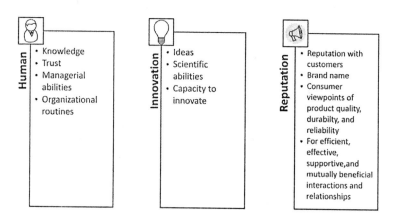

Human
- Knowledge
- Trust
- Managerial abilities
- Organizational routines

Innovation
- Ideas
- Scientific abilities
- Capacity to innovate

Reputation
- Reputation with customers
- Brand name
- Consumer viewpoints of product quality, durabilty, and reliability
- For efficient, effective, and mutually beneficial interactions and relationships

Organizations depend on intangible resources as core competencies because they are not easily discernable and more difficult replicate or substitute for. The more "invisible" a resource is, the better the competitive edge based on it. Intangible resources can be leveraged, unlike tangible resources. Take knowledge for example. People can share knowledge without reducing the value of the resource and in fact, could make the resource even more valuable. Reputation is also an excellent intangible resource. Reputation indicates the level of brand awareness an organization has been able to build amongst its consumers and how highly the consumers think of the organization.

It is generally believed that intangible resources are much more valuable as core competencies than tangible because they are typically what makes an organization unique.

Capabilities

Integrating resources for a specific task or tasks produces capabilities. Building capabilities usually happens over a period of time through complicated activities between intangible and tangible resources. Capabilities frequently come from employee skills and knowledge that is unique to them. Capabilities are also actions that an organization performs remarkably better than competitors. Unique value is added to an organizations products and services through capabilities as well. Typically, you can find capabilities in the following functional areas:

a) Distribution

b) Human resources

c) Information systems

d) Marketing

e) Management

f) Manufacturing

g) Research and development

The following table demonstrates some examples of what unique capabilities can emerge from these functional areas.

Functional Area	Capability
Distribution	Effectively utilizing logistics management policies and procedures
Human resources	Effectively motivating and retaining employees
Information systems	Use of point of purchase data collection methods to effectively and efficiently control inventories
Marketing	Innovative merchandising and advertising
Management	Ability to successfully envision the future of the industry
Manufacturing	Exception product and design quality
Research and development	Ability to quickly transform technology into new products and processes

Core Competencies

Core competencies are the source capabilities of competitive edge an organization has over their competitors. They typically emerge over time and help to differentiate an organization and demonstrate its nature. If we look at all of an organization's resources and capabilities, we will find that only a few of them are strategic assets. Strategic assets are assets that potential sources of competitive advantage and have some sort of competitive value. Some of the assets could prove to be a detriment to the organization because they shine a light on areas that the organization is weaker in. There isn't a magic number of core competencies that an organization is required to have in order to have the competitive advantage. However, most effective strategic plans can be built around three to four competencies. There is caution in having too many core competencies because organizations tend to lose their focus on the core competencies that can really give them the upper hand over competitors.

When recognizing and developing core competencies, organizations usually use the standards for a supportable advantage and/or value chain analysis. When we are determining our competitive advantage, we want to make sure that it is something that can be maintained and lost easily. Using the criteria of usefulness, uniqueness, expensive replication, and no viable alternatives helps us to decide can we afford to maintain this advantage? Does it make sense? The value chain analysis allows organizations to determine which core competencies should be invested in to be maintained since they are creating value for consumers. The value chain also helps us to map out the process, so we can understand what areas might benefit from being outsourced.

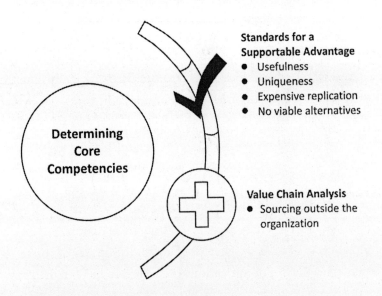

Standards for a Supportable Advantage
- Usefulness
- Uniqueness
- Expensive replication
- No viable alternatives

Determining Core Competencies

Value Chain Analysis
- Sourcing outside the organization

Standards for a Supportable Advantage

Core competencies should meet these four criteria:

a) **Usefulness** – how useful is it and does it have real value? Can it be used to reduce threats and create opportunities?

b) **Uniqueness** – specific to an organization itself, no other organization owns it

c) **Expensive replication** – is the cost of replicating the product too high to make it worth it?

d) **No viable alternatives** – there are no alternatives out there that can take its place

Capabilities that do not meet the four criteria are not core competencies. The table below gives you a better idea of what happens when all criteria are not met.

Is it useful enough to present a threat to competitors?	Is it unique enough to give us a competitive advantage?	Is the cost of replicating the product too high to be worth it?	Are there any other alternative solutions out there?	Is there a competitive advantage?	Is there a competitive disadvantage?	What does performance look like?
No	No	No	No		✓	Less than average
Yes	No	No	Yes/no	Competitive parity		Average
Yes	Yes	No	Yes/no	✓ But temporary		Average and possibly slightly above average
Yes	Yes	Yes	Yes	✓		Above average

Value Chain

The ability to be able to identify areas of operation that do and do not add value is referred to as the value chain analysis. This is an important piece to understand because an organization's profit potential increases when the value they create is more than the costs they incur. The value chain is a template that is used by organizations to clarify their cost position and direct the implementation of a specific business-level strategy through primary and support activities. Primary activities in the value chain bring the product to the consumer. These activities would include creating the product itself, selling and shipping it to buyers, and providing customer service after the sale. Support activities are assistance activities that occur to make sure that the primary activities happen. The most valuable piece in the value chain as a whole are people who have the knowledge of their consumers.

Let's look at the primary activities in the value chain a little closer. Below are the primary activities defined:

a) **Inbound logistics** – Actions that are utilized to receive, store, and distribute inputs to a product

b) **Operations** – Actions that convert the inputs into the final product.

c) **Outbound logistics** – Actions that include gathering, storing, and shipping out the product to consumers

d) **Marketing and sales** – Actions to entice consumers to purchase the product and providing outlets for the consumers to purchase from.

e) **Service** – Action that boost or preserve the value of the product

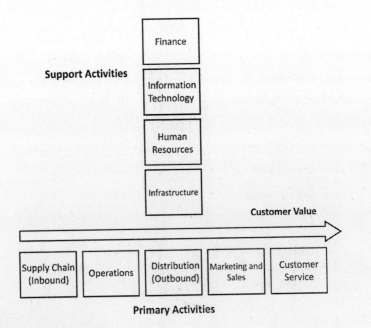

Value Chain - Primary Activities

Using the Value Chain

The first step in using the value chain is to identify the primary activities of the value chain for your organization. The next step is to identify sub activities for each primary activity that helps to create value. There are different types of sub activities:

a) **Direct** – creates value by itself

b) **Indirect** – assists direct activities in running easily

c) **Quality assurance** – helps to make sure that both direct and indirect activities are meeting standards of quality.

Next, ask the question, what are the activities that fall under of the support activities? Out of all of the primary activity sub activities, which ones generate the most value? Essentially, you are following the lower level activities through the value chain and detailing what the value add is and if it is significant. After these step, determine if the sub activities are direct, indirect, or apply to quality assurance. Are there other activities that are value adds that are part of your organization's infrastructure? If so, capture those as well. They may not be related directly to a primary activity and you will also want to determine if they are direct, indirect, or related to quality assurance.

Fourth, ask the question, "How are all of these activities related?" Once you begin to answer this question, you begin to piece together your organization's competitive advantage from a value-chain viewpoint. For example, there is a link between sales force training and sales volumes.

Finally, ask yourself the question, "How can I improve or maximize the value my organization gives to the consumer with our products and services?"

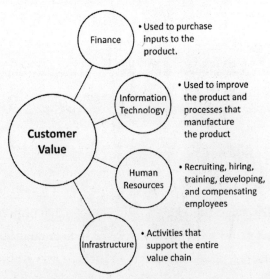

Value Chain – Support Activities

A few important things to remember when identifying your organization's value chain:

a) Align proposed changes with your organization's overall business strategies.

b) Determine a process and prioritize your list.

c) This process gives you a big picture perspective. For a more in-depth look, conduct a value chain analysis.

Value Chain Analysis

A value chain analysis includes three steps:

a) **Activity analysis** – what activities do you complete to provide your service?

b) **Value analysis** – what can your organization add to these activities to provide the highest value to the consumer?

c) **Evaluation and planning** – examine the list of things you developed from step 2 and determine if completing the change would add enough value to be worth the work.

The activity analysis step includes brainstorming with your team or organization to list all the actions you take that add value or enhance your consumer's experience. Taking this from a top-down approach, you can first consider what this looks like from an organization level. An example of actions that the organization takes that adds value is the defined business process that are used to provide service to the consumer. These actions an include marketing, operations procedures, distribution, and customer support. If you look at this from an individual or team level, the actions would be the ones you do on a day to day basis that carry out the work you do. Also, be sure to include everything that adds value, not just the obvious daily activities to provide the product. For example, activities like motivating team members, recruiting a skilled workforce, or research and development on the latest technologies.

An important thing to remember about this brainstorming activity is that you will get more ideas and better answers if you brainstorm with a team rather than just brainstorming by yourself. Also, going through the exercise and coming up with ideas will encourage better buy in from team members regarding the proposed changes you come up with out of the exercise.

After you have generated your list of activities from brainstorming, identify correlating "Value Factors" with each item. Value factors are things that your consumers place value on due to the method each activity is completed. Let's look at a doctor's office for example. One of the things on your list may be the nurse call process. Your consumer probably puts a high value on how quickly the nurse answers the phone or calls them back, how polite they are, and how knowledgeable they are. After you have identified the value of each activity in your list, examine what could be modified to give an even greater value to the consumer.

The last step is to look at the modifications you have listed and develop a plan for the next steps to be taken. The previous step will result in a long list of activities that would be great if you could complete all of them. It is important to take a moment and think through how you will complete the changes you have listed and accomplish what you set out for in a timely manner. Instead of going down the list in the order in which you listed them, take time to prioritize. Pick the low hanging fruit first. These activities are ones that are easy and quick to complete. Look through the remainder of the list and ask, "Is this change worth it?" and "what is the real value-add at the end of the day?" Remove items from the list that require a large work effort and little value add. Then, prioritize the rest of your list in a way that will allow a steady pace of achievement and add value to keep both team members and consumers excited about your organization's products and solutions. Another option for assistance in prioritizing the list is to consult with a customer you work closely with to get their input on the list regarding what would be most valuable.

Outsourcing

When an organization purchases a value adding activity from a supplier that is external, they are outsourcing. Outsourcing allows organizations to be more flexible, alleviate risks, and decrease their investments in capital. More organizations are turning to outsourcing because they cannot obtain the resources and capabilities necessary to reach a competitive advantage in every primary and support activity. Outsourcing allows organizations to focus on the core competencies they really excel at.

If you intend to get involved in outsourcing at your organization, it is critical that you have the following skillsets: tactical thinking, negotiating, partnership authority, and change management. You need to be a strategic thinker because you must understand your organization's core competencies and how an outsourcing partner could help your competitive edge. You must be able to make deals or negotiate with outsourcers, so they can be used by organization management. You should be empowered to oversee and manage the relationship with the outsourcer. Finally, utilizing outsourcing can require a large amount of change so it is very important that you are able to manage change.

The biggest downfalls of outsourcing are the growing concerns from communities regarding the loss of jobs for local workers to outsourced companies. There is also a possible risk of loss capability to effectively innovate. When considering outsourcing at your organization, you should be sure to plan for these concerns from consumers and employees and be ready to discuss it.

There are also advantages to outsourcing. It can possibly decrease costs and improve the quality of the actions that have been outsourced. By doing this, you add value to the products and services you provide to the customer. Therefore, outsourcing can result in a competitive advantage for an organization and allow value to be created for its stakeholders.

Case Study

Let's look at Apple as a case study for determine strengths and weaknesses. Apple is a household name. Most consumers have heard of Apple the company are aware of some of items they produce such as the iPhone. This awareness is called brand awareness and it is probably one of the biggest strengths of Apple. They also have a strong brand identity. Consumers may describe their products as aesthetically pleasing and creative. The Apple brand can also be described as a status symbol. iPhones are coveted by consumers because they associate them with an extravagant or wealthy lifestyle. They are willing to wait for hours on end just to obtain the newest version of the phone.

What are Apple's weaknesses? First, their products are costly which definitely eliminates some consumers. The population who can afford their products are narrowed by their price point. The high price of their product is part of the prestige that is a strength, but it does affect them negatively by limiting the number of consumers that can purchase their product.

Chapter **4**

External Analysis

The external analysis of the organizational environment allows you to determine the organization's opportunities and threats. Opportunities are described as an opportunity to exploit an external condition that will improve the organization's strategic competitiveness. A threat is just the opposite. A threat is a condition in the general environment that could detrimentally affect an organization's strategic competitiveness.

When you are completing an external analysis, you are collecting and analyzing data on the industry, national environment, and the socio-economic environment. During this analysis, we are concerned about the competitors in the industry and their position as well as our position in the industry. We are also looking at how the environment as a whole could affect us and our long-term planning including economic, social, governmental, legal, technological, national and international factors.

Let's continue with the Apple case study and look at their external factors. An opportunity externally that Apple has demonstrated time and time again is their unique ability to be able to effectively and efficiently collaborate with other companies. They have collaborated with companies that produce popular headphones to create a wireless Airpod product. They have also worked with gaming companies to have games specially created for the iPhone. On the flip side of opportunities, are threats. A huge threat that Apple faces is the large amount of imitation that occurs in the marketplace. Companies produce products that are similar to Apple products and a lower price point. Competition is also a big threat for Apple. Companies like Samsung advertise that their products have just as much functionality, if not more, at a lower price point, with less hassle and cost of future upgrades.

Environments - General

When completing an external analysis, you should consider three environments:

a) General
b) Industry
c) Competitor

The general environment is described as broader societal dimensions that influence an industry its organizations. These dimensions are divided into seven segments including:

a) Demographic
b) Economic
c) Political/Legal
d) Sociocultural
e) Technological
f) Global

g) Physical

Please refer to the table below for more detail on the elements included in these dimensions. In order to create successful strategic plan, organizations should be knowledgeable of these dimensions.

Demographic	Population size
	Age structure
	Geographic distribution
	Ethnic mix
	Income distribution
Economic	Inflation
	Interest rates
	Trade deficits or surpluses
	Budget deficits or surpluses
	Personal savings rate
	Business savings rates
	Gross domestic product (GDP)
Political/Legal	Antitrust laws
	Taxation laws
	Deregulation philosophies
	Labor training laws
	Educational philosophies and policies
Sociocultural	Women in the workforce
	Women in the workforce
	Attitudes about quality
	Concerns about the environment
	Shifts in work and career preferences
	Shifts in preferences regarding product and service characteristics
Technological	Product innovations
	Applications of knowledge
	Focus of private and government-supported R&D expenditures
	New communication technologies
Global	Important political events
	Critical global markets
	Newly industrialized countries

	Different cultural and institutional attributes
Physical	Energy consumption
	Practices used to develop energy sources
	Renewable energy efforts
	Minimizing an organization's environmental footprint
	Availability of water as a resource
	Producing environmental friendly products
	Reacting to natural or man-made disasters

It is important to note that the general environment cannot be controlled by organizations. Therefore, companies that are successful in this environment have a deep understanding of the segments, gather the appropriate data and analyze it, and then account for what they find in their strategies. Organizations are influenced by the current states of the segments.

When organizations study the demographic segments, they try to take into account the global climate due to possible effects in different countries since organizations may compete in global markets. When analyzing the economic segment, we are considering the where the economy is now and where it is going. Examining this segment helps to plan to meet a general goal of most organizations which is to compete in an industry that is relatively stable with potential for growth. The political/legal segment learn about the relationships between organizations and the government. We look at how they impact each other in the current state and how future state might be impacted so we can plan accordingly. Society's values, attitudes, and cultural views are taken into accounting the sociocultural segment. These things can actually affect how the demographic, economic, political/legal, and technological segments behave and evolve. Innovation with new products, processes, and resources is the focal point of the technological segment. This segment includes developing new learning's and converting that knowledge into products, services, resources, and processes. The global segment looks at new and current markets, how they are changing, pertinent international events, and critical cultural qualities. Finally, the physical segment is focusing on supporting the environment. Organizations have begun to gain a clearer understanding of how the physical environment can influence business practices, so they include this segment to plan accordingly.

The industry environment that organizations refer to can consist of things like demographics, shifts in lifestyle and economic cycles per businessdictionary.com. It includes Porter's Five Forces: risk of new competitors, power of suppliers and buyers, risk of duplication, and intensity of competitor rivalry. The key to this environment is to find a position in the market where your organization can positively influence the forces or successfully protect themselves against their influence. This is particularly helpful in volatile industries like the airline industry where there is intense rivalry amongst competitors and getting pushed out of the industry is relatively common even for the industry's leaders.

Gathering information about other competitors in the industry and analyzing that data is referred to as competitor analysis and is used to understand the competitive environment. Competitor analysis couple with the information from industry and general environment analysis give organizations a great big picture of what they are dealing with. General environment analysis focuses on forecasting the future. Industry environment analysis is pinpoints the influences on an organization's profitability potential within its industry. Looking at analysis on competitors helps us understand how competitors may act in the future so that your organization can respond appropriately.

In an effort to better manage and comprehend the current environment, organizations conduct external environmental analysis. This analysis is comprised of four segments: scanning, monitoring, forecasting, and assessing.

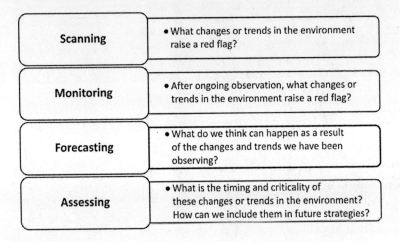

There are many sources that can be referenced when you are collecting data on the general environment. Those sources include:

a) Trade publications

b) Newspapers

c) Business publications

d) Academic research

e) Public polls

f) Trade shows

g) Suppliers

h) Customers

i) Employees

Scanning

The first step in the external environmental analysis process is scanning. Scanning involves looking at all segments in the general environment. Scanning often results in early signals of possible changes and helps to identify any changes that are already happening. This part of the process is a data gathering activity. You collect raw data from several different sources but how the information is related is still unclear and often incomplete. It is important that the scanning activities are in alignment with the environment. For example, the scanning system for a stable environment should be calibrated for stable environments not volatile environments.

Today, organizations often utilize software specialized to identify these changes and trends. This software is set up to look for specific pieces of information which can sometimes cause a false alarm. Organizations are willing to take the tradeoff of this software raise false alarms if it increases the probability of early detection of red flags. Another way to detect changes is by using capabilities in internet browsers that allows organizations to collection information about those who click through their sight.

Monitoring

At this step, researchers are sifting through the data gathered to determine what pieces are meaningful. After determining this, they begin to actively monitor the changes and trends to see if something worthwhile that could affect their strategies is happening in the environment. To be effective in monitoring, organizations must accurately identify their stakeholders and know what their standing is amongst those stakeholders. Understanding this allows organizations to meet the needs of their unique population they serve. Industries with high technological ambiguity find scanning and monitoring particularly critical. It gives them information, develops new knowledgebase items about the environment, and helps them determine the best strategies for marketing their new technologies.

Forecasting

After monitoring the trends and performance of the current environment, analysts gather the information and use it to help them determine what could happen in the future and when. For example, analysts may forecast how long it will take the government to put a particular regulation in place or how quickly a competitor is bringing a new technology to the consumer. Technology is improving at such a rapid rate, that it often expedites the product life cycle which, in turn, makes accurate forecasting difficult. Therefore, the greatest challenge in forecasting is accuracy. If you are unable to forecast close to accurate, your potential profitability could be affected. For example, Company A forecasted a 22% increase in sales for 2017 but the increase was actually 32%. Your first reaction may be positive since we sold even more than we had anticipated. But, the supplies for your products were ordered in quantity to support a 22% increase in sales. Company A found itself in a situation where they had more demand than supply due to not estimating for the larger increase. This did affect profitability because the company was unable to sell as much as what the customer was demanding.

Assessing

We have collected the data, pieced it together and determined what pieces are meaningful and what is not. Now, understanding the timing and significance of the effects of the changes and trends on strategic management is important. The organization is now postulating the effects of the things they have learned on the organization itself. The key thing to remember here is that how the data is interpreted is paramount. If the interpretation of the information gathered is incorrect, inadequate strategies are developed and the organization profitability is affected. Many companies gather the data and organize but they do not assess it to see what it means to them. In these cases, they are increasing their risk of an inaccurate strategy implementation. Assessing ensures that the proposed strategy is correct.

Environments – Competitive

After completing an industry analysis described in an earlier chapter, the last piece of external analysis is a competitor analysis. In this analysis we are looking at every company that your organization competes with. This analysis is most interested in the competitor's objectives, strategies, assumptions, and abilities. In this analysis, we want to know:

a) **The competitor's driving force** – what objectives do they want to reach in the long term?

b) **The competitor's current state** – what are their current strategic plans?

c) **The competitor's industry beliefs** – what do they believe to be true regarding the industry?

d) **The competitor's abilities** – where is the organization strong and where is the organization weak?

Having this information allows an organization to determine how to respond.

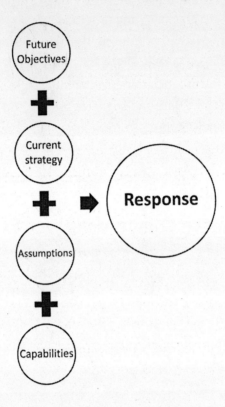

When an organization considers future objectives, they are looking at:

a) In comparison to our competitors, what do our goals look like?

b) In the future, where should we place the most importance?

c) How risk averse are we?

When an organization considers current strategy, they are looking at:

a) Currently, how are we competing?

b) Are changes in the competitive structure supported in their strategies?

When an organization considers assumptions, they are looking at:

a) Are we assuming a volatile or stable future?

b) Is status quo how we are functioning?

c) What are the assumptions that our competitors hold when they look at the industry and themselves?

When an organization looks at capabilities they are looking at:

a) Where are we strong and weak?

b) If we were to rate us and our competitors, where do we fall in the list?

Using the answers to these questions we can determine a response that answers the following questions:

a) Our competitors are likely to do (fill in the blank) in the future.

b) What do we have to offer over our competitors?

c) Does this change our relationship with our competitors? How?

Case Study

Let's take a case study of a successful environmental scanning example and an unsuccessful environmental scanning example.

PepsiCo

PepsiCo, popular soft drink and beverage manufacturer completed an environmental scan and found that health and wellness is becoming a big part of the food and beverage industry today as well as other industries. The CEO took this to heart and began developing a long-term strategy to include health snacks and beverage alternatives in their portfolio of products. The CEO has a goal of tripling their healthy products business by the year 2020. The company decided to use an acquisition strategy to get them into the health and wellness market more quickly with already successful products such as those manufactured by Naked. They also have increased the research and development budget related to healthier ingredients that can be backward engineered into their current products.

PepsiCo made the right decision at the right time to move with the industry quickly. Other companies have suffered because they did not do appropriate planning to incorporate health and wellness.

Borders

Borders filed for bankruptcy in 2011 due to poor environmental scanning and not taking action on what was returned from environmental scanning analysis. Despite reports of a growing internet presences from other stores in the industry and an increased use of online purchasing outlets, Borders chose to invest in its CD business and its physical book business instead of focusing on beefing up their internet presence. Environmental scanning also indicated that digital downloads were on the up rise for CDs as well as eBooks for books. Due to their lack of reaction to these environmental trends, they were forced out of business. This is definitely an example of poor management of environmental scanning and its analysis.

Chapter **5**

Formulation of Strategy

After completing an internal and external analysis, organizations begin formulating their strategies. During this step they are answering questions like:

a) Knowing what we now know, how do we want to move forward?

b) How can we best succeed in meeting our goals and objectives?

During this formulation phase, organizations develop strategies on various levels in the organization.

Strategy Levels

As mentioned earlier, the goal of developing strategies is to determine how our organization can plan to triumph in a time period in the future. In order to disseminate organizational strategies, we need to have few different levels of strategy. There are three levels of strategy:

a) **Business** – the department's strategic plan for helping to meet the corporate level strategy

b) **Corporate** – organizational level strategy setting the big picture for where the organization is going

c) **Team** – the individual team's strategy for how it will add value to corporate and business strategies

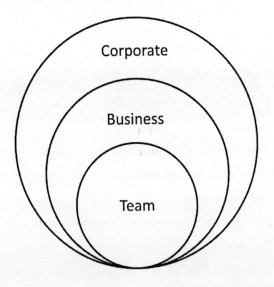

The focus of any strategy is to gain a competitive edge and increase potential profitability. A good strategic plan is backed by the organization's vision and mission statement. You can look at the strategic plan and understand, based on the vision and mission, why these actions make sense for this organization. Effective strategies details how the organization's resources, capabilities and competencies will be utilized. Decisions outlined as part of the strategy seek to decrease ambiguity in outcomes.

Business Level Strategy

Business level strategy seeks to do all of the things described above but it is focusing on a departmental or unit level and doing it in particular product markets. This strategy reflects the decisions that have been made regarding competing in discrete product markets. The business level strategy gets you closer to the consumer. It states who your consumers are, what their needs are, and how the unit will meet those needs. Defining these things can prove to be challenging considering increased participation in the global market.

Business level strategies have a direct relationship with the consumer. If you consider that the consumer is the life force behind your organization, it is in the organization's best interest to meet those consumer needs in order to increase the organization's returns. If you cannot keep the consumer satisfied, you cannot stay in business.

Managing Customer Relationships

A common strategy of many successful organizations is to focus on innovative methods to please current consumers and, hopefully at the same time, satisfy new consumers. To achieve the goal of satisfying customers, organizations spend a good amount of time managing these relationships, so they have a better handle on current and future requirements. Customer relationships should be managed from a three dimensions standpoint since there are three dimensions to managing customer relationships. These dimensions are reach, richness, and affiliation.

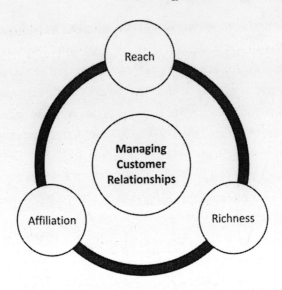

Reach refers to the organization's access and association with consumers. A great example of reach is with Amazon.com. Amazon.com gives consumers access to millions of different products and they reach the consumer through tens of millions of computers across the world. Although Amazon.com is not a brick and mortar store, its reach is more extensive than most other stores such as Barnes and Noble.

Richness is related to the bidirectional flow of information between the consumer and organization. Specifically, what is the complexity and detail of the flow? Improving the richness dimension helps organizations institute a competitive advantage which is the reason increasingly more organizations are utilizing the internet and online services to help better manage the flow of information. They are also using it to supply the consumer with a knowledgebase about their products and solutions, so they can be better informed on how the organization can meet their needs. Use of these online methods has considerably reduced information interchange costs for consumers and organizations.

The final dimension, affiliation, refers to assisting productive exchanges with the consumer. An example of this would be Autotrader.com. Autotrader.com offers an online service, as well as an app, which allows consumers to find information on cars and compare their features and costs. Consumers are given the flexibility to sort the information and filter the information to suit their needs. It even connects the consumer with suppliers in their area and assistance with financing investigation. This process creates a tremendous value for the consumer because they can go one place to get all the information they need instead of several different places and it is no cost to them.

Who Do We Need to Satisfy?

In order to have an effective business level strategy, we must understand who our target consumer is. Organizations use market segmentation to divide consumers into groups according to similarity in needs. This exercise is useful in several different situations. For example, the needs for catering services for individuals is different than the needs for catering services for companies. Groups can be formed off of just about any identifiable characteristic but there are ones that are commonly used by organizations in market segmentation.

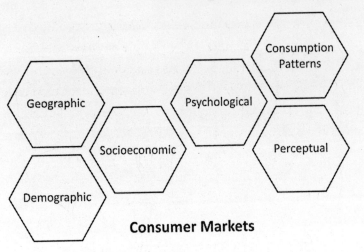

Consumer Markets

For consumer markets, there are several factors that are commonly used to segment the market. Demographic factors can be used to segment groups by age, income, sex, etc. It can also be used to divide consumers into generational groups with particular interests or desires. Socioeconomic factors can include the social class, stage in the life cycle of a family, etc. Geographic factors are cultural, regional, national differences, etc. Psychological factors can include lifestyle, personality traits, etc. Consumption patterns refer to consumers that utilize the product heavily, moderately, and lightly. Perceptual factors are things like benefit segmentation and perceptual mapping.

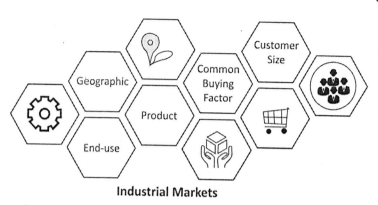

Industrial Markets

There are also several common segments used to divide an industrial market. End-use segments are segmented by Standard Industrial Classification (SIC) codes which classifies industry areas. These SIC codes help to reflect the end use of the product. Product segments are centered on technological differences or manufacturing economies. Geographic segments look at boundaries between countries or by regional discrepancies between them. Common buying factor segments consider groups of people who may think that the same buy factors are significant. Customer size segments divides things into groups by account size or geography.

What Consumer Needs Are We Satisfying?

After determining our target audience, we now look at what their specific needs are that we need to satisfy. Generally, customer needs are focused on benefits, features, or performance of the product. Organizations that are most effective are able to give consumers what they request, when they request it. The best way to understand the consumer's needs are through frequent interactions. At a high level, consumers are looking for a product that adds value for them. In terms of defining value, consumers are either looking for low cost with adequate features or high quality with tolerable cost. Most organizations strive to get ahead of the consumer demands because failure to do this can result in a loss of consumers.

How Will We Satisfy the Consumer's Needs?

If you remember from earlier reading, core competencies give organizations a competitive advantage. Organizations utilize these core competencies to develop value adding strategies and meet consumer needs. Continuous improvement, innovation, and promotion of an organization's core competencies is key to meet consumer needs and, hopefully, go above and beyond in the future.

Business Strategy Purpose

Business level strategy seeks to create dissimilarities between the organization and its competitors. Organizations want to set themselves apart from competitors and in order to do this, they must determine if they want to complete activities in a different way or complete dissimilar activities. Making this decision really determines the organization's business level strategy which is a choice made by the organization about how they will utilize the organization's value chain actions to establish a value that makes them standout. Business level strategy, in essence, seeks to create a competitive advantage. Typical sources for creating this competitive advantage are:

a) Having lower costs than competitors

b) Performing actions differently

c) Delivering a product that costs less and is consider acceptable by the consumer

d) Obtaining the capability to make the organization's product stand out so much that it commands a top price

e) Carrying out higher valued activities

Five Levels of Business Strategy

Common strategies used at the business level to set apart organizations from their competitors are cost leadership, differentiation, focused cost leadership, focused differentiation, and integrated cost leadership/differentiation. Each strategy develops a competitive advantage by varying its scope. Although the strategies are generally the same at any organization, the variance occurs with how each organization integrates their strategic actions.

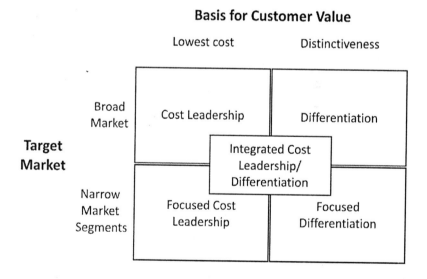

Basis for Customer Value

	Lowest cost	Distinctiveness
Broad Market	Cost Leadership	Differentiation
Narrow Market Segments	Focused Cost Leadership	Focused Differentiation

Integrated Cost Leadership/ Differentiation

Target Market

Cost Leadership

In the cost leadership strategy, the goal is to have the price be the competing factor. The organization works on lowering their costs, so they shift that value to a wide customer base. In order for this strategy to be sustainable, you must have internal efficiencies that result in above average margins. Organizations using this strategy typically have top of the line facilities and low costs. Control over overhead and production costs is tightly managed. This strategy works well for generic products or standardized products. Keeping a low cost is a continuous effort with this strategy so you can beat the competition. To obtain an edge over the competition, organizations must determine and control cost. They also should examine what reconfigurations can be done in the value chain to lower costs. Risks of this strategy are technology could become obsolete, competitors able to imitate successfully, and tunnel vision on cost leadership resulting in loss of consumer perception of product differentiation. This strategy's usefulness in relation to the five forces is listed below.

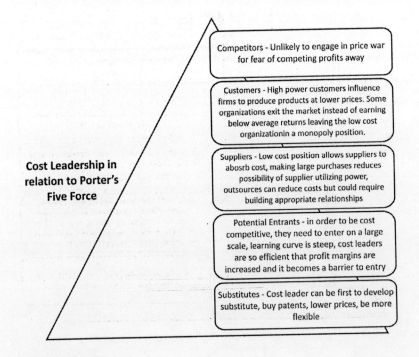

Cost Leadership in relation to Porter's Five Force

Competitors - Unlikely to engage in price war for fear of competing profits away

Customers - High power customers influence firms to produce products at lower prices. Some organizations exit the market instead of earning below average returns leaving the low cost organizationin a monopoly position.

Suppliers - Low cost position allows suppliers to abosrb cost, making large purchases reduces possibility of supplier utilizing power, outsources can reduce costs but could require building appropriate relationships

Potential Entrants - in order to be cost competitive, they need to enter on a large scale, learning curve is steep, cost leaders are so efficient that profit margins are increased and it becomes a barrier to entry

Substitutes - Cost leader can be first to develop substitute, buy patents, lower prices, be more flexible

Differentiation

This strategy focuses on delivering a product that is very unique. So unique that the price of the product is not an issue. In differentiation, high quality, speedy innovation, and superior customer service are characteristics. In this strategy, value is created by lowering the buyer's costs for repairs, increasing the buyer's performance by improving the performance of the product, and sustainability with high switching costs. Risks of this strategy are difference between cost leader and differentiator becomes too large, value of the differentiation diminishes, experiences with the product narrows consumer's viewpoint of uniqueness, organizations successfully imitate product at a lower cost. This strategy's usefulness in relation to the five forces is listed below.

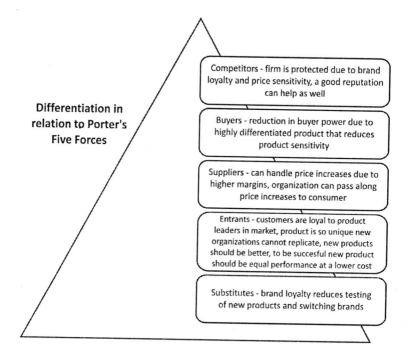

Differentiation in relation to Porter's Five Forces

Competitors - firm is protected due to brand loyalty and price sensitivity, a good reputation can help as well

Buyers - reduction in buyer power due to highly differentiated product that reduces product sensitivity

Suppliers - can handle price increases due to higher margins, organization can pass along price increases to consumer

Entrants - customers are loyal to product leaders in market, product is so unique new organizations cannot replicate, new products should be better, to be succesful new product should be equal performance at a lower cost

Substitutes - brand loyalty reduces testing of new products and switching brands

Focused Strategies – Focused Low Cost and Focused Differentiation

Focused strategies use a low-cost or differentiated strategy, but the scope is narrowed. Scope can be narrowed by particular buyer group, segment of a product line, or geographic markets. To utilize a focused strategy, you must be able to complete value chain actions in an exemplary way to keep the competitive advantage and generate above average returns. Organizations may use this strategy for several reasons including to serve an underserved niche of the market, lack of resources for broader market, better effectiveness, and focus resources to improve specific value chain activities. Risks of focused strategies include being out focused by a competitor, large competitor finds the market segment attractive, and the consumer changes their preferences.

There are two types of focused strategies: focused lost cost and focused competitive advantage. The focused low-cost strategy has a competitive advantage of low cost and a serves a narrow market. Focused differentiation continues to differentiate their product by making its features unique, but the product is only offered to a small targeted market. Using this approach allows the organization to serve the customer in a very efficient way. This is a risky approach in that there is a likelihood that the targeted population loses interest, or a competitor finds the target market enticing.

Integrated Low Cost Differentiation

This strategy attempts to provide the best of both worlds where the products are low cost and unique. The organization learns new technology and exploits the organization's core competencies to provide this product. This strategy is flexible to external environmental changes. The value chain needed for this strategy must have competence and flexibility built in. The flexibility in this strategy generally comes from flexible manufacturing systems (FMS), information technology, or total quality management (TQM) systems. FMS is a computer-controlled process line used to generate products in flexible quantities requiring little intervention. The goal of this system is to produce a lot of product at a low cost. Information technology helps to speed up the process and produce higher quality products. It enhances the work flow between the organization and the suppliers. TQM utilizes continuous improvement by empowering employees to problem solve during their processes. It increases customer satisfaction, lowers costs, and reduces time to market. It is a great way to maintain competitive advantage but by itself it is not a competitive advantage. The risk of the integrated low-cost differentiation strategy is that the product stays in limbo meaning that they do not offer the consumer enough value in relation to low cost or differentiation.

Dynamics of Competition

An organization's actions are dynamic when competing. One organization may lower their prices and in response a competitor lowers their prices. Competitors are continuously reacting to each other's strategy in the market. In fact, some organizations, in their strategic planning, try to anticipate the other competitor's reaction and will deliberately do something to elicit a desired response from a competitor. As we discuss competitive rivalry and competitive dynamics there are some definitions you should be aware of.

Competitors	• Organizations offering the same or similar products in the same market to the same consumer
Competitive Rivalry	• The way individual competitors act, respond, and react to other competitors while working to obtain a more advantageous market position
Competitive Behavior	• The way competitors act, respond, and react while building, defending, or improving their market position
Multimarket Competition	• Organizations that compete with each other in many product or geographical markets
Competitive Dynamics	• The complete set of actions and reactions that all organizations take while they are competing against each other in a market

These definitions all relate to each other and the competitive process. Take a look at the diagram below to get a better understanding.

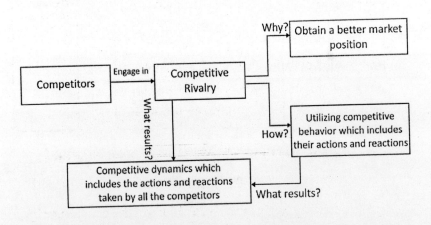

The process above has a great impact on the success of a strategy. Success is determined by the initial actions of an organizations, an organization's ability to anticipate other competitor's reactions to them, and an organization's ability to anticipate and react to other competitor's initial actions. Rivalry has an impact on all strategies with the strongest influence on the business level strategy.

Rivalry Model

Organizations are equally interdependent. One organization's actions have obvious effects on its competitors. Organizations will deliberately act to elicit a specific reaction from its competitors. Competing organizations are continuously impacting each other's actions and reactions. Rivalry at this level is typically dynamic and multifaceted. The function of success in any market is a result of both individual strategies and their consequences. The model below demonstrates how competitive rivalry works.

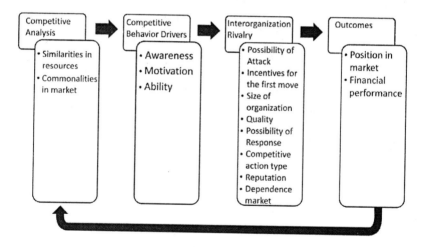

Feedback

Competitive rivalry begins with an analysis of the competitor by looking at their awareness and drive to act aggressively or respond to competitive actions. The possibility of action or response results in outcomes where outcomes are controlled by the organizations capability to take strategic action. Feedback from the outcomes comes back to affect future competitive dynamics with an impact on the competitive behavior drivers. The level of intensity of the competitive rivalry in a market is usually grounded in the possibility of response from competitors. Considering this, competitors usually are not interested in taking action on a competitor that will retaliate.

Competitor Analysis

Remember from earlier reading that competitive analysis is completed to help organizations understand their competitors by examining strategies, future goals, assumptions, and abilities. Completing this analysis allows organizations to better predict and anticipate their competitor's actions so they can prepare possible responses and reactions.

The major things to examine in competitor analysis are market commonality and resource similarity. Understanding if there is a high or low market commonality and resource similarity allows organizations to determine the extent to which organizations are competitors. For example, Sprint and Verizon have a high market commonality and resource similarity indicating that they are direct competitors. Although the competition between these two is fierce, direct competitors do not always have an intense rivalry.

Market commonality looks at how many markets are an organization and a competitor participating in and how significant each individual market is to each competitor. When organizations competing against each other compete in multiple markets, they are participating in multimarket competition. Organizations that participate in multimarket competition are not as likely to initiate aggressive action but if they are attacked, they will react aggressively.

Resource similarity refers to how similar competitors' products, tangible and intangible, are in relation to types and amounts.

Firms with a high resource similarity will likely have like strengths and weaknesses and utilize like strategies. Analyzing resource similarity is more difficult when the essential resources are intangible.

Competitive Behavior Drivers

Market commonality and resource similarity influence the three competitive behavior drivers:

a) Awareness

b) Motivation

c) Ability

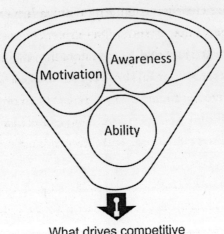

What drives competitive
behavior?

The drivers also impact the organization's competitive behavior demonstrated by actions and reactions it utilizes while participating in competitive rivalry.

Awareness happens before any organizational action or response and it is the degree that a competitor is familiar with the level of their mutual interdependence that comes from their competitive analysis. When organizations have very similar resources they utilize while they compete in multiple markets, the awareness tends to be high. The more aware an organization is of its competitors, the better the understanding of the consequences of their competitive actions and reactions. When the awareness is low, there is extreme competition which negatively effects all of the competitors' performance.

Motivation is described as the organization's incentive to act or react to a competitor's attack in relation to seeming gains and losses. If an organization believes that their market position could be negatively impacted, and their market position would reduce favorability due to inaction, their likelihood to act is increased. The same holds true for the reverse. Motivation and market commonality are closely related. An organization's likelihood to attack a competitor that it has a high market commonality is lower whereas if there is a low market commonality, the likelihood his high. The main reason for this type of relationship is due to the high risks involved with attacking a rival that an organization competes in multiple markets with. This results in a high probability that the competitor will retaliate if action is taken on them.

Ability is referring to each organization's resources and the agility these resources offer. If some organizations do not have available resources, the ability to attack a competitor and react to a competitor's actions are reduced. If an organization has similar resources to that of a competitor, close examination and planning of a possible action on the competitor must be completed since that competitor is likely to react to that action. As the resource dissimilarity between competing organizations increases, so does the delay of reaction by the organization that has lesser resources. Opting to not respond to a greater resourced competitor's attack, can result in failure of the organization so a response should always be attempted no matter how challenging it may seem.

Strategic and Tactical Actions

Actions taken by organizations when they are engaging in competitive rivalry are both strategic and tactical. In order to better understand the actions taken, there are a few definitions to be familiar with.

Competitive Action
- Action taken to develop or defend an organization's competitive advantages or better its position in the market

Competitive Response
- Action taken in opposition to that of a competitor's action

Strategic Action or Response
- Actions that are market based involving a large commitment of resources with increased difficulty to implement and reverse

Tactical Action or Response
- Actions that are market based taken to tweak an organization's strategy that usually involves fewer resources and is easy to implelment and reverse

Possibility of Attack

There are additional drivers used to predict the possibility of a competitor attack in addition to market commonality, resource similarity, awareness, motivation and ability. These drivers are:

a) First mover incentive

b) Organizational size

c) Quality

First Mover, Second Mover, Late Mover

A first mover is just as it sounds. It is an organization that takes the first move (or competitive action) to develop, improve or protect their position in the market. Organizations that are first movers typically have funds allocated for advanced product research and development, assertive advertising, and innovation and development. The advantage of being a first mover is customer loyalty and market share that is difficult for competitors to gain. First movers usually start with groundwork of higher research and development. They are experimenters with new innovations and are typically very assertive. They are risk takers and can tolerate a higher level of risks that are reasonable. They also usually have an abundance of liquid resources that they can easily allocate when they want to take action. Learning curve is step due to the new innovations but benefits can be worth it.

The second mover is the organization that reacts to the first mover's aggressive action. They are typically more risk averse than the first mover. They take time to study the consumer's responses to product innovations. They also keep track of lessons learned from the actions of the first movers to reduce their risk. More efficient than the first movers, the second mover takes more time to test new processes and technologies to help reduce costs. The benefits of being a second mover are not as high as the first mover and the returns are lower.

Late movers take their time in responding to competitive action and wait until after the first and second movers take their action. Achievements by late movers are slower in arriving and are not as high as those of the first and second movers. Late movers' returns are only average and understanding the value creation for the consumer is delayed as well. Risks are lowest as a late mover, but returns are very low as well.

Organizational Size

Organization size plays a part in predicting possible competitive attacks. Small organizations usually have a greater likelihood of acting aggressively in competitive environments. They are usually faster to act and more agile. They also enjoy the elements of surprise and speed when they are defending their position. Their agility allows them to have more choices in competitive actions than larger organizations.

Large organizations will likely act aggressively in competitive environments and strategically take action. Their resources are greater. Unlike the small organization, they have a limited number of choices of competitive actions to take which can adversely affect their competitive advantage. The ideal organization has the best of both worlds. The organization has the resource slack of a large organization and the agility of a small organization. It is crucial for success that organizations not rely on limited types of competitive actions because it can result in reduced success over time. Remaining agile will allow you to use a variety of competitive actions which will support future success.

Quality

From a strategic point of view, quality occurs when an organization's products or services meet or go beyond the consumer's expectations. Quality is a necessary evil because without it, an organization lacks credibility, but quality alone does not equal competitive success. Ultimately, quality is the end results of an organization's primary and support activities. Top level leadership must support any quality effort and endorse its importance throughout the organization and the value chain. Consumers judge quality based on a variety of dimensions. They will typically compare the quality of one organization's product to its competitors. Below is a list of the quality dimensions for products and services.

Product Quality Dimensions
- Performance - how well the good operates
- Features - critical characteristics of the good
- Flexibility - Ability to meet operating specifications over time
- Durability - how long the product can be used before it deteriorates
- Conformance - how well the product match to the pre-established standards
- Serviceability - how easy and speedy repair is
- Aesthetics - how appealing the product is to the senses
- Perceived quality - consumer's subjective assessment

Service Quality Dimensions
- Timeliness - does it perform in the promised time period?
- Courtesy - Is it performed happily?
- Consistency - do all customers have the same experience each time?
- Convenience - how accessible it is to customers
- Completeness - is it serviced as required?
- Accuracy - is it performed accurately every time?

Additional Factors

There are more factors that organizations look at to estimate how a competitor will respond to competitive action. Those factors are:

a) Type of Competitive Action

b) Actor's Reputation

c) Dependence on the Market

General rule of thumb is that an organization will most likely respond when competitive action greatly reinforces, or delay abates the organization's competitive position. Success of competitive action is affected by the likelihood and effectiveness of response.

Type of competitive action is different with strategic action and tactical action. In general, strategic actions garner strategic reactions and tactical actions garner tactical reactions. If you look at what is involved with strategic action, you understand why fewer strategic actions are launched and reacted to than tactical actions and reactions. Strategic actions require significantly more resources and is more difficult to reverse than tactical action. Also, strategic action is not taken and implemented lightly therefore, there is a delay in reaction to competitive strategic action. Oppositely, tactical action is likely to be responded to quickly by competitors.

An actor refers to an organization acting or reacting to competitive response. Reputation refers to the positive or negative characteristics that each competitor has based on past behavior. As organizations get ready to take action, they study competitor's previous history of responses to better predict a likely response. When a market leader takes competitive action, competitors are more likely to respond. In fact, if a strategic play is successful for an organization, it is likely it will be imitated and used again.

Dependence on the market refers to the degree that an organization's revenues or returns are consequent from a specific market. Organizations that are highly dependent upon the market are more likely to respond more aggressively to actions that threaten their market position. Response may not be swift, but organizations know that their response must be successful in order to thrive.

Competitive Dynamics

Rivalry in competition refers to the continuous actions and reactions between an organization and its direct competitor for a desirable market position. In contrast, dynamics in competition refers to the continuous actions and reactions among all competitors that are competing in the market for desirable positions. Organizations must build and maintain their competitive advantages because it is key to generating value for the shareholder. Different types of markets elicit different types of competitive behaviors. Dynamics are different in slow cycle, fast cycle, and standard cycle markets. The ability to maintain competitive advantage is also different across the three market types. The level of sustainability varies by type of market and is affected by how rapidly competitive advantages can be counterfeited and how much it costs.

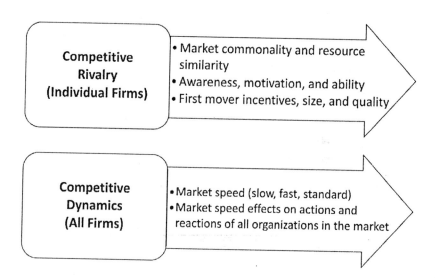

Slow-cycle Markets

In slow-cycle markets, imitation is limited and costly, so competitive advantages are guarded. Sustainability is another characteristic of a slow cycle market. To be successful in a slow cycle market, you must develop a distinctive and branded capability that provides a competitive advantage lending to sustainability. Once this is done, behavior should focus on guarding, sustaining and spreading that advantage. To effectively support strategic work, utilize your organization's structure. Look at the diagram below to see what the competitive dynamics produced by organizations competing in slow cycle markets.

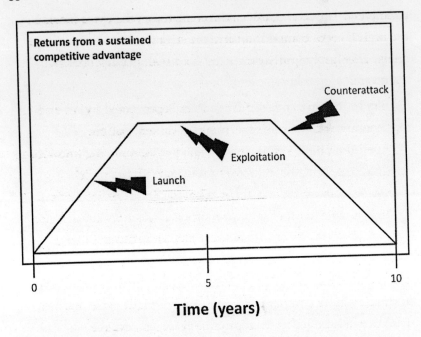

Time (years)

In a market that is slow-cycle, a proprietary product is launched with a competitive advantage. Then, it is exploited for as long as it is guarded from other competitors. After a while, other organizations react to the product launch with an aggressive action.

Fast-cycle Markets

A fast-cycle market refers to a market where the organization's competitive advantage is not guarded from replication. Replication in these markets is typically fast and inexpensive. Therefore, competitive advantages are very difficult, if not impossible, to sustain in a fast-cycle market. The technology is not proprietary. Speed is key in fast-cycle markets to enable an organization to keep a market position. Top managers are continuously pressured to make strategic decisions rapidly and effectively. The strategic decision is intricate when you factor in the high level of competition and the strong technology strategic focus. This just heightens the need for a really comprehensive approach.

Speedy imitation in a fast cycle market is promoted by reverse engineering and the rate of technology dissemination. Competitors utilize reverse engineering to develop the knowledge needed to replicate or improve products. With the rapid technology dissemination, technology to create the products is made available to other organizations in a short period of time. This technology is typically not patented or protected like it is in slow-cycle markets. Unpredictability is a characteristic of a fast-cycle market, in fact, fast-cycle markets have the highest level of unpredictability compared to slow and standard cycle markets. The pace of innovation in this market is rapid because organizations depend on them for growth. Prices tend to decrease rapidly so profit from new product innovations must happen very quickly.

In fast cycle markets, a competitive advantage is nearly impossible to maintain. Organizations are not loyal to any one product and are willing to cannibalize their own products to bring new ones live before competitors do. Short term and temporary competitive advantages are utilized in fast-cycle markets and are typically not kept for long. Organizations move from one temporary advantage to another in the hopes of outrunning their competitor's responses to their strategic actions.

Take a look at the competitive behavior of fast-cycle markets in the diagram below.

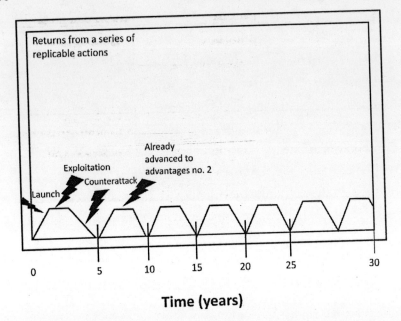

Standard-cycle Markets

Standard-cycle markets refer to markets where the organization's competitive advantages are shielded at a medium capacity from replication and where replication is moderately costly. There is some hope in maintaining competitive advantages in this market, but it will only happen if the firm is flexible enough to continuously elevate the quality of its abilities and therefore making the advantages dynamic. Competitive behavior in this market is designed to obtain large market shares, win consumer loyalty with a highly respected and recognizable brand name, establish economies of scale, and closely monitor operations to ensure the same positive customer service experience every time. Competition is usually pretty intense in standard-cycle markets because competitors compete in markets all over the world. Innovation is a driver in competitive behavior and innovations are not always radical in this market either.

	Imitation	Competitive Advantage
Slow-cycle Markets	• Slow and costly • Proprietary • Expensive to imitate • Capability is developed from unique historical conditions, casual ambiguity, and /or social complexity	• Sustained competitive advantage is most achieved in this market
Fast-cycle Markets	• Rapid and inexpensive	• Not sustainable • Can be reverse engineered
Standard-cycle Markets	• Faster and less costly than slow-cycle markets • Slower and more expensive than fast-cycle markets	• Partially sustainable

This page is intentionally left blank

Chapter 6

Corporate Level Strategy

In this section, we examine corporate level strategies which seeks to answer the question, "What product markets and businesses should we compete in?" It also helps to define how the corporate headquarters should manage those businesses. Corporate level strategy is the top-level strategy for the entire organization. The purpose of a corporate level strategy is to assist the organization in earning above average profits. This strategy dictates the actions taken by an organization to gain a competitive advantage. It seeks to increase the organization's value by choosing new strategic positions.

There are several different strategies we will examine including:

a) **Product development** – launching new products or significantly improving current ones

b) **Market development** – launching in new geographic

markets

c) **Horizontal integration**–merging with or purchasing competitor organizations, moving horizontally at a specific point in the value chain

d) **Vertical integration** – merging with or purchasing suppliers or distributor so the organization can now be its own supplier or distributor, moving vertically up or down the value chain

Diversification Levels

Diversification is a common corporate level strategy where organizations utilize their excess resources by venturing into new business areas that are either related or unrelated. A diversified organization has both a corporate level and business level strategies and usually a business strategy for each business. The opposite is true. Organizations that are not diversified and are vested in a single product market are likely to have one corporate level strategy and one business level strategy. Diversified organizations tend to have many business level strategies and maybe more than one corporate level strategy.

Organizations that are diversified vary in their level of diversification. The common levels of diversification seen in organizations are listed below. Value creation in diversification comes from sharing resources and transferring core competencies across different businesses. Decisions makers must exercise caution when motivated to diversify because some of organization's value can be destroyed if there is not careful planning.

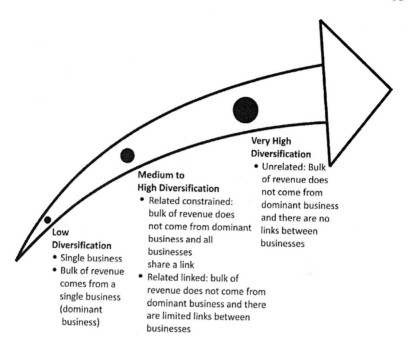

Very High Diversification
- Unrelated: Bulk of revenue does not come from dominant business and there are no links between businesses

Medium to High Diversification
- Related constrained: bulk of revenue does not come from dominant business and all businesses share a link
- Related linked: bulk of revenue does not come from dominant business and there are limited links between businesses

Low Diversification
- Single business
- Bulk of revenue comes from a single business (dominant business)

As you consult the illustration above, you see that an organization is related through its diversification when there is shared linkage across products, technologies, and channels of distribution. As the links amongst the business increase, the relatedness of diversification becomes more and more constrained. When the links decrease to the point of having no links at all, the businesses are unrelated.

Product development/diversification is a commonly used corporate level strategy that looks at the scope of the markets where the organization competes. Ideally, a diversified portfolio balances costs and benefits. It does this by keeping profitability steady from profits from all of the different businesses. Again, agility is key because organizations need to position themselves where they can shift their investments to the markets with the most returns when needed.

Elementary diversification level includes working on a single business plan and the dominant business diversification strategy. The single business plan consists of an organization that makes more than 95% of its sales from its main business. An example of a single business plan organization is Wm. Wrigley Jr. Company, they make bubble and chewing gums. The foremost business diversification approach consists of an organization that makes 70-95% of its sales within a single business area. An example of this strategy is seen with the United Parcel Service.

The next level is moderate to high level diversification including related constrained and related linked diversification strategies. This strategy entails less than 70% of revenue coming from the main business and products, technologies, and channels of distributions are shared amongst the businesses. There are several examples of these types of strategies today such as Proctor & Gamble, Johnson & Johnson, and Campbell Soup. Related linked diversification strategy again has less than 70% of sales coming from the main business and the linkages are mixed. This means that the business share fewer resources, but they do conduct knowledge transfer of competencies among the businesses. An example of a moderate to high level diversified organization is GE.

Very high levels of diversification indicate that the business is unrelated. The main business does not generate more than 70% of sales. An example company would be Samsung.

Creating Value with Diversification

An organization utilizing a diversification strategy adds value for its shareholders when linking expertise and resources of the companies fulfills one of the following circumstances:

a) Larger profit or value from the two companies working together vs. an investment in the individual companies.

b) A decrease in the inconsistency of the revenues better than what could be appreciated from a group deal in the two companies. Essentially you are diminishing the risk for the system.

Operational Relatedness and Corporate Relatedness

There are many reasons an organization may choose to diversify. The diagram below shows the different reasons commonly used.

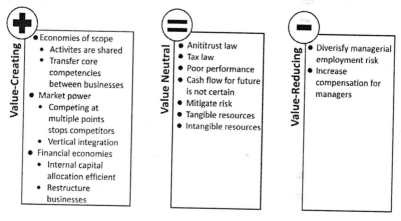

Value-Creating
- Economies of scope
  - Activites are shared
  - Transfer core competencies between businesses
- Market power
  - Competing at multiple points stops competitors
  - Vertical integration
- Financial economies
  - Internal capital allocation efficient
  - Restructure businesses

Value Neutral
- Anititrust law
- Tax law
- Poor performance
- Cash flow for future is not certain
- Mitigate risk
- Tangible resources
- Intangible resources

Value-Reducing
- Diverisfy managerial employment risk
- Increase compensation for managers

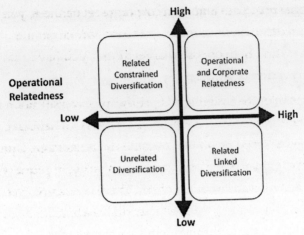

Corporate relatedness

Remember that the way an organization creates value is by developing or extending their resources, capabilities and core competencies. Value is created in the form of cost savings when organizations utilize economies of scope. This is where organizations reduce costs by sharing resources and capabilities or transferring core competencies. Usually, organizations look to create economies of scope by either operational economies/operational relatedness or corporate relatedness. As you look at the illustration above, you see a map for when certain diversification strategies create value by looking at operational relatedness and corporate relatedness. Operational relatedness is the extent to which we share activities between businesses. Corporate relatedness is the extent to which we transfer core competencies between businesses. If you have a high level of corporate relatedness, it is said that you are utilizing horizontal related diversification. If you have low operational readiness and low corporate relatedness, you have unrelated diversification. This would mean that your organization is pursuing a conglomerate diversification strategy where you obtain unrelated businesses in an effort to increase cash flow. If you have low operational readiness and high corporate relatedness, you have related linked diversification. If you have low corporate relatedness and high operational readiness, you have related constrained diversification.

The purpose of the different value creating diversification is to gain market power from competitors. When this happens, economies of scope result and becomes an advantage. Operational relatedness gain economies of scope by sharing in primary and support activities in the value chain. There is risk involved with operational relatedness because sharing the activities also means that the outcomes are linked. Operational relatedness is challenging to implement because you are coordinating multiple activities across multiple value chains in multiple businesses. Often there are synergies that are not realized as planned.

Corporate relatedness focuses on transferring core competencies between businesses. These competencies typically involve managerial and technological knowledge, experience and expertise. There are two sources of value creation in corporate relatedness. Because the first business incurs the expense and initial knowledge is generated there, the resource allocation for the second business is less. Knowledge, for example, is an intangible resource so this gives the organization an immediate competitive advantage since this knowledge is difficult to understand or imitate. Transferring knowledge can be done by simply moving a key employee to a new position. There is risk involved with this move because you are moving valuable information out of its current area into a new one.

Market Power

Market power refers to an organization that has the advantage of selling their products above the current competitive level or they can reduce costs of primary and support activities below the current competitive level. They may even be able to accomplish both tasks. This typically relates to related constrained or related linked diversification. Related diversification strategies involving market power include vertical integration and virtual integration. Vertical integration happens when a company can produce its own inputs. That is referred to as backward integration.If they distribute their products themselves, they are said to be forward integrated.

Virtual integration is a new to value chain management. In this scenario, the value chain links are brought together by informal agreements with suppliers and consumers. This is heavily reliant on It because the shipments of supplies or products to or from the organization are all organized through the internet or other networked system in this approach.

Another way organizations can create market power is through multimarket competition which is when multiple diversified organizations all compete in the same product and physical location markets. Typically, in multimarket competition you see a reduction in competition intensity due to frequent contact between organizations. This condition is also known as mutual forbearance. Generally, price wars are avoided and barriers to entry are lower.

Operational Connections and Corporate Connections

When operational connections and corporate connections happen at the same time, it creates economies of scope sharing activities and transferring core competencies. Comprehending and replicating this is very challenging. In order to achieve this, you must have operational and corporate forms of economies of scope. Implementation of this approach frequently fails due to multiple issues. In order to provide value, the cost must offset the benefits of this approach. If this does not occur, you create diseconomies of scope.

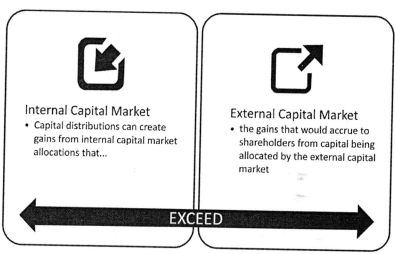

Internal Capital Market
- Capital distributions can create gains from internal capital market allocations that...

External Capital Market
- the gains that would accrue to shareholders from capital being allocated by the external capital market

EXCEED

Unrelated Diversification

Unrelated diversification focuses on adding value by being fiscally responsible and frugal. First, investments inside or outside the organization allow rough improved distributions of financial resources and therefore cost savings. Second, restructuring or selling the organization can allow for cost savings or even achieving above average profits.

In unrelated diversification, there is a focus on allocating capital efficiently in the market economy. Investors hold equity positions with high forecasted future cash-flow. Debt holders work to improve the value of their investments by taking risks in businesses with high growth and profitability prospects.

A conglomerate discount is also used. This discount is incurred when analysts are uncertain how to value a large array of big organizations with complex financial reports. Stock markets will apply this discount of 20% on unrelated diversified firms which indicates that they belief is that the value of the conglomerates is 20% less than the value of the sum of its parts. To get past this discount, some organizations have worked to create a brand for the parent company.

Unrelated diversification has its pitfalls. Most importantly, being fiscally frugal is easier to replicate than operational and corporate relatedness. In up and coming markets, this is less of an issue because existence of services that are needed to keep up the economic, health, and social standards of the population is not there. Unrelated diversification strategy is promoted due to this absence. The next step is to diversify in up and coming markets and begin seeing improved performance of largely diversified organizations.

Restructuring of Assets

Financial economies are created with restructuring. Organizations will buy a company, restructure it, and then sell the company's assets in the external market. Economic downturns can present opportunities to buy more companies, but it also can present some risks. An example of this risk may be purchasing a company that is in such poor order, even restructuring will not make it profitable. In order for restructuring of assets to be successful, organizations should look for mature, low technology companies that are not reliant on client orientation.

Value Neutral Diversification

Not all diversification creates value. There are other incentives to diversify that an organization may choose to take advantage of even though it does not create value. Incentives are external and internal. The external incentives include antitrust regulations and tax laws. Internal incentives include low performance, uncertainty of future cash flows, and synergy and risk reduction.

Antitrust regulation has distinct impact on market actions. In the 1960s and 1970s, antitrust regulated mergers that created large amounts of market power. This action discouraged the strategy all together. Conglomerates started to pop up because vertical and horizontal mergers were no longer viable options. In the 1980s, vertical and horizontal mergers became options again as regulations were loosened. In the late 1990s, merger activity boomed as deregulation occur in specific industries. In the early 21st century, antitrust regulations rear their ugly head and possibly mergers are closely controlled.

Just as antitrust regulation had an impact, so do tax laws. Buying and building businesses in high performing markets increases when dividend taxes increase. In 1986, the Tax Reform Act reduced individual income tax by almost half the rate. Ordinary income now had capital gains included. Shareholders began focusing on investing in dividends instead of acquisition because the act dissolved some of the corporate tax advantages of diversification.

When organizations are largely diversified, they tend to not perform as well as those that are less diversified. Often, organizations feel the need to diversify due to low performance so if they are performing well, there is no urgent need. Organizations performing poorly are willing to put all of their chips on the table and undergo riskier activities in an effort to turn their business around.

Some organizations use diversification as their strategy for defending their market position. When a product line seasons or is vulnerable, it may be time for a diversification defensive strategy.

When an organization is small and in a budding industry, diversification may also be a good option to consider. If there is concerns about future cash flow performance, diversification could be an option to consider.

To be able to realize the synergies between business units, you must have flexible investments. Synergy is, essentially, the sum being greater than its parts meaning that all of the organizations work together add more value than they do individual. With this synergy taking place, all of the units that make up the "sum" are dependent upon each other. So, if one-piece stops working, then the value received by all parts in the process is reduced or diminished. Reduce the risk of issues with the technological piece of synergy by operating in environments that are more certain and not constantly requiring change. As organizations try to maintain their synergies, they may become more risk averse. It loses the possible synergies and ultimately creates more unrelated diversification.

Value Reducing Diversification

When top level leadership in an organization diversify, they typically do it to reduce their own employment risk if it does not adversely affect profitability. Top level leaders reap the advantages of this diversification, but shareholders do not receive any value. Therefore, the government has put mechanisms in place to keep this in check. Managers are incentivized to diversify to reduce their risk and increase their compensation.

Chapter 7

Mergers and Acquisitions

Mergers and acquisitions (M&A) strategies have been trending for many years. Today, these strategies are growing in popularity in countries overseas. These strategies help organization quickly grow and achieve above average profitability. These strategies played a large role in the 1980s and 1990s with restructuring and continue to prove beneficial today. The external environment has a huge impact on merger and acquisitions due to tight credit markets and political changes in foreign countries' familiarity with the strategy. In the most recent financial crisis, organizations found it difficult to complete big deals with other organizations due to the tight credit market. In 2011, big deals between organizations became more popular and volume rose by 45%. When there are currency imbalances, cross border acquisitions pick up because the country with the stronger currency can purchase the organizations in the country with the weaker currency. Mergers and acquisitions is a great strategy to create value for all shareholders. The value created applies to all level strategies.

There are several reasons that an M&A strategy is used. Usually it is used to address the uncertainty in the competitive market. Using this strategy, organizations can increase market power due to competitive threat, share risk, move core business into other markets, and manage industry and regulatory changes. The purpose is to increase an organizations strategic competitiveness and value. However, it doesn't often work as plan and returns are usually zero. Creating value is definitely a challenge with the M&A strategy.

The upside to an M&A strategy is that the shareholders of the acquired organizations usually earn above average returns from the acquisition. The down side is that shareholders of the organizations that are purchasing other businesses earn zero return. And, more than half of the time, the stock price falls after the acquisition is announced. This response is typically a sign that investors are skeptical as to whether the synergies will really be realized.

Let's look at the definitions for some of the key terms we will be discussing in this section.

Merger

- Two organizations integrate their operations on an equal basis
- True mergers are few and far between because their is usually a dominant organization in the transaction

Acquisition

- An organization purchases 100% interest in another business with the goal of making the business a subsidiary within its portfolio

Takeover

- This occurs when an organization acquires another business that did not solicit their bid

Hostile Takeover

- Aggressive takeover that is not wanted by the target business

A hostile takeover does not sound like a desired strategy, however, the reasoning behind it is that when the announcement is made that the hostile takeover is occurring, the share price for the bidder and target organizations increase in price.

As mentioned earlier, acquisitions are risky and often are not successful. Considering this, why even go with the acquisition strategy? The following diagrams give you the reasoning behind doing an acquisition strategy and why there are issues with success.

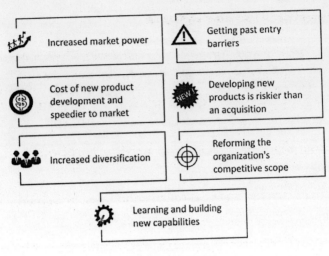

Why acquire?

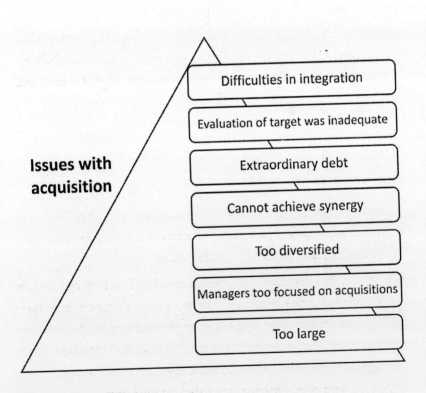

Issues with acquisition

Difficulties in integration

Evaluation of target was inadequate

Extraordinary debt

Cannot achieve synergy

Too diversified

Managers too focused on acquisitions

Too large

Increasing Market Power

Leading in the market provides market power. There are several factors that increase market power including:

a) Ability to sell products or services above the competitive level

b) Costs of primary and support activities are below competitors

c) Advantage to size of the organization, resources, and capabilities and share of the market

d) Purchasing a competitor, supplier, distributor, or a business in a highly related industry allows sharing of activities

Market power can be increased by horizontal acquisitions, meaning purchasing another business in the same industry. An example of this would be if Starbucks acquired Caribou Coffee. The increase in market power occurs when synergies in cost and revenue are realized. And, if the organizations have similar characteristics, the performance is higher.

Vertical acquisitions are also a market power increaser because the organization is essentially buying their suppliers or distributors. An example of this would be if a medical device organization purchased a third-party vendor that sold their devices. The organizations market power is increased when they are able to control additional parts of the value chain.

Finally, related acquisitions, where organizations buy businesses in related industries increases market power. Value creation takes place in this strategy when the synergy developed by integrating resources and capabilities is realized. The downside to this strategy is that synergies are historically difficult to implement therefore, you rarely see many related acquisitions.

Any acquisitions that are done to improve market power are subject to regulatory review and financial market analysis.

Barriers to Entry

Getting past market barriers to entry is another reason companies look at completing acquisitions. The common entry barrier reasons organizations choose to acquire are:

a) Economies of scale

b) Differentiated products

Purchasing an established company can be a more effective strategy to entering a market rather than trying to fight the uphill battle of economies of scale and differentiated products. As a matter of fact, when the barriers to entry are high the probability is high that that an organization will acquire another company. Using acquisition to enter a market is expensive but is a good way to get immediate access to a market.

Cross Border Acquisitions

When an organization purchases a company that has a headquarters in another country, they are acquiring across borders. In cross border acquisitions, the purchaser has more control over international operations as opposed to a cross border alliance. Organizations in the United States have been actively practicing cross border acquisitions for many years. Currently, more and more countries globally are beginning to choose this option as a way to get into a market. In Europe, regulations are relaxed which has resulted in an increase in cross border acquisitions. In the late 1990s both European and U.S. organizations conducted cross border acquisitions with Asia during their financial crisis. Many analysts believe that these acquisitions helped Asia to recover.

Producing New Goods and Speediness to Market

It is a very costly investment to create new goods and introduce them into markets. It is so costly that returns are difficult to obtain early on. When returns are not gained, new products cannot continue to be developed and introduced. It becomes a vicious cycle if you do not have good planning. Contributing to this failure is the ability to replicate a similar product at a lower price within just a few years of introduction to the market. Due to these high stakes, managers often feel that new product development is a very risky activity.

Acquisitions provide an alternative strategy to get new products into new markets. Acquisitions allow for faster market entry and better returns. Organizations can also easily predict future returns by looking at past performance. Considering that the technology is a very dynamic industry with a constant need for the newest and best thing, in order for these organizations to stay afloat, many of them turn to acquisition.

New Products are Higher Risk

The risk involved with acquisitions is lower than that of developing new products. Outcomes are more easily predicted by looking at past performance than looking at outcomes of creating a net new product. Acquisition strategies are often used to avoid risky internal undertakings and risk investments in research and development. Ultimately, acquisitions could become an alternative to innovative so therefore it should be treated as a strategy and not a defensive move.

Organizations that seek to change their portfolio of businesses with diversification use acquisitions because it is the quickest and easiest way. Increasing relatedness between organizations that are going through acquisition equates to a greater probability of a successful acquisition.

Reforming Scope

When there is intense competitive rivalry, an acquisition can help to reduce the negative effects on financial performance. It can also diminish the organization's dependence on a specific product or market. When you decrease this dependence, you change an organization's competitive scope.

New Capabilities

Acquisitions can allow organizations to gain capabilities they currently don't have. Capabilities such as special technology, broader knowledge base, and reduced inertia are examples of capabilities more easily obtained through acquisition. To best build its own knowledge base, organizations should acquire companies that have related and complementary capabilities.

Issues

Integration

After an acquisition occurs, integration of the two organizations must take place. This is a very difficult task to successfully complete. Things like molding together two cultures, combining different financial and control systems, rebuilding working relationships between organizations, and resolving issues as they arise particularly with organization executive leadership. Many benefits have been identified from completing acquisitions, but it also has its share of disadvantages. Although an acquisition can add value, it does not mean it is without issues. Less than a quarter of all M&As are successful and more than half produce results that are undesirable. Less than a quarter of all M&As are complete failures where technology acquisitions have even higher rates of failure.

Steps to a successful acquisition are:

a) Choose the right target company

b) Negotiate as low a price as possible to avoid paying a high premium

c) Ensure integration of operations of both organizations is effective

d) Keep the target company's people

There are several commonly seen issues that organizations see while attempting to integrate the two organizations. First, one of the hardest things to do is to somehow mold together to distinctly different corporate cultures. Finding a common ground between the two and still maintaining part of the acquiring organization's culture is a daunting task. The change involves people to change behaviors which is one of the hardest things to accomplish because most people do not like change.

Other issues commonly seen include integrating the two financial and controlling systems. These systems are often technological systems that need to be either integrated together or data moved from one system to another. Careful planning is crucial for this task because data integrity and an employee learning curve can be highly impacted.

Not all acquisitions are contentious in nature. Many are amenable. Even in those situations, building effective working relationships can be a challenge especially when each person has a different management style and every organization has different management philosophies. Again, careful planning is required for this task because it involves an organization's most important resource – people. This piece also includes determining how to proceed with the executives from the companies acquired. Do you keep them in leadership roles temporarily to help in building these relationships or do you immediately displace them to another role or outside the organization? These resources can be valuable in helping to keep the relationships building effectively. They can also be a liability if the person is not on board with the acquisition.

While integrating the two firms, be prepared to lose some key employees. Organizations that have carefully planned and seemingly have done everything right, still lose some of their top performers. The impact of this is a reduction in the firm's capabilities and reduced value while the organization seeks new employees, onboards, and trains them.

Poor Targeting

When an organization is considering acquiring a company, a process called due diligence is followed. Due diligences is a process where the company is evaluated for purchase. During this process, organizations often look at the financing of the transaction, cultural differences, tax consequences, complexity of combining two workforces, current financial position, quality of the fit, and ability to effectively integrate. If this due diligence is not performed effectively, an organization could end up paying an excessive amount for a company.

Debt

In the 1980s and 1990s, when acquisitions were occurring frequently, several companies increased their debt. Junk bonds were invented during this time which made the increase in debt possible. Junk bonds are a way to finance risk acquisitions with money that provides a large possible return to lenders. Not only do junk bonds increase debt, they increase the possibility of bankruptcy. They can affect the organization's credit rating detrimentally. They also detrimentally affect investment in activities that could improve the organization's long-term success such as research and development, training, and marketing.

Unrealized Synergy

Synergy happens when the value of the organizations working together is greater than the value of the organizations working independently. Synergy happens when economies of scale and scope occur because the two organizations are sharing resources. Using acquisition to create synergy can have its downfalls. Organizations can incur transaction costs and often, indirect costs are underestimated when completing due diligence.

Real competitive advantage with synergy occurs when a transaction creates private synergy. Private synergies occur when the two organization integrate, and they are able to develop capabilities and core competencies that they could not develop on their own. This type of synergy is very difficult for competitors to duplicate and understand. However, it is also difficult for the organization to recreate it as well.

Over diversification

Another reason for the inability to reach success with acquisitions is too much diversification. Over diversification happens at varies points in an organization but depends upon how much capacity they have to manage the diversification. Organizations that are diversified must process more information of greater diversity. The operational scope can become so big that managers focus too much on financial controls instead of strategic controls to tell them how their business units are performing. Strategies change focus to the short term instead of long term. At this point, acquisitions may become an alternative to innovation.

If you recall from previous discussion, related diversification has more information processing requirements than unrelated diversification. Due to this requirement, these organizations can become over diversified with less business units than unrelated diversifiers. In over diversification, performance declines, and business units become divested. Even if an organization has not reached the point of over diversification, they can be negatively impacted in the long term.

Over Focus on Acquisition

Acquisitions can become unsuccessful if management is too focused on it. Managers over focus on acquisitions because the thrill of the deal is more exciting than running the company itself. During the acquisition process, they spend a lot of time and energy on finding viable target companies, effectively completing due diligence, preparing for negotiations, and integrating companies after the acquisition is completed. Managers also put a pause on critical decision making for fear that it can affect outcome of the negotiation. Acquisition can force management to shift to a short-term focus and become more risk averse.

Size

Finally, when an organization is too large, additional costs and management complexity can cause the benefits of an acquisition to become less worth it and result in diseconomies of scope. When organizations are too big, there is more bureaucracy in decision making. The upside to this is that there is more consistency in decision making. The downside is that organizations can often become rigid in management. Less innovation may also result in large organization.

What Makes an Acquisition Successful?

Now that we have an idea of the pitfalls of acquisitions, let's look at what makes an acquisition effective.

Start by examining the list below.

Attributes of Successful Acquisitions

a) Organization to be acquired has complementary assets or resources

b) Friendly acquisition

c) Effective and thorough due diligence conducted

d) Organization acquiring has cash or a favorable debt position

e) Acquired organization has low to moderate debt

f) Consistent focus on research and development and innovation by the acquiring organization

g) Change is managed well and is flexible and adaptable

Results of Successful Acquisitions

a) Increased possibility of synergy and competitive advantage

b) Quickly and effectively integrate with a possibility of lower premiums

c) Organizations with strongest complementarities are acquired and there is no overpayment

d) Financing is easily attainable and less costly

e) Lower financing cost, lower risk, and avoidance of trade-offs related to high debt

f) Sustain long term competitive advantage

g) Quickly and effectively integrate resulting in realized synergy

In order to have a successful acquisition, an organization should have an effective strategy in place. The following strategies most often lead to a successful acquisition.

Complementary Assets/Resources	Purchasing organizations with assets that meet current needs to build competitiveness
Friendly Acquisitions	Integration goes smoother when the deal is friendly
Due Diligence/ Careful Selection Process	Careful and deliberate evaluation and negotiations lead to better integration and realized synergies
Maintain Financial Slack	Have enough resources financially that profitable projects can be capitalized on.

There have been instances historically where an acquisition as enhanced strategic competitiveness. However, in the 1970s to 1990s, this was not the case. When this happens, as it very often does, the organizations use restructuring to correct the failure.

Restructuring

Restructuring is a way for a business to change its businesses or financial structure. This often occurs after an unsuccessful acquisition or changes in the internal or external environment. Some of the restructuring strategies include downsizing, down scoping, or leveraged buyout.

Downsizing occurs when there is a reduction in the number of organization employees and its operating units, but the core of the business does not change. This strategy is tactical and short term with a goal to cut labor costs. You typically see this strategy used when the acquisition failed to create the expected value, or the organization paid too much for the target. Downsizing could change the composition of businesses in an organization's portfolio. The most common reasons for downsizing are to improve profitability from labor cost decrease or a need for more efficient operations.

Down scoping consists a divestiture, spinoff, or other way to eliminate a business that is not related to the organization's core business. This is a strategic move and is long term. It focuses on the core businesses of the organization and reduces portfolio diversity. It has a more positive effect on the organization performance than downsizing. This strategy may be done in tandem with downsizing, but key employees should not be displaced. This allows a smaller organization to be more effectively managed by the leadership team.

Down scoping is most commonly used in U.S. countries. In Europe, Latin America and Asia, building conglomerates has been a growing trend. In Asia and Latin America, some of the focus of conglomerates has been shifted to western corporate strategies where they focus on their core businesses. Competition has been enhanced globally by down scoping in tandem with globalization and market liberalization.

Leveraged buyout occurs when another party buys all the business assets, financed mostly with debt, and makes the organization private. This strategy is most commonly used to correct management mistakes or correct mistakes made by managers who were focused on serving their own interests. A private equity organization means that the organization is taken private on the stock exchange. When this occurs, large amounts of debt may be incurred to pay for the buyout. Immediately, the organization begins to look at selling non-core assets to start to drill down some of the debt. There are three types of leveraged buyouts:

a) Management buyouts

b) Employee buyouts

c) Whole-firm buyouts

Typically, management buyouts lead to down scoping, a better strategic focus, and increased performance. You see this more with management buyouts than employee or whole-firm buyouts. Organizations choose leveraged buyouts as a viable strategy because it protects them against an unpredictable financial market. It allows organizations to focus on developing innovations and bringing them to market. It also facilitates entrepreneurial efforts.

There are downsides to leveraged buyouts. First, the organization's financial risk is increased due to their large debt.

Also, a short term and risk averse managerial focus occurs to avoid detrimentally affecting the transaction. This causes a reduced investment in research and development. Leveraged buyouts usually occur in industries where stable cash flows are possible, and the industry is mature.

Typical outcomes from restructuring are listed in the diagram below.

Downsizing	Downscoping	Leveraged Buyout
Short Term Reduced labour costs **Long Term** Loss of people Lower performance	**Short Term** Reduced labour costs Greater focus on strategic controls **Long Term** Higher performance	**Short Term** Greater focus on strategic controls High costs of debt **Long Term** Higher risk

Case Study

Let's take a look at an automobile manufacturer A&M for a real-life example.

In 1994 BMW chose to acquire Rover Company, a British automobile company. Rover Company started by building bikes and motorbikes then eventually moved into producing cars. BMW is a German automobile, and motorcycle manufacturer. It actually began as an aircraft engine company.

BMW was incentivized to purchase Rover because they wanted to grow. Rover was a desirable target because they had developed a significant cost advantage because it use Japanese production procedures. They also wanted to get into front wheel drive and 4X4 manufacturing which Rover currently had in production. According to critics, BMW got a great deal because the technology and product methods were light years apart from what they were currently using and stood to provide them a great amount of efficiency and cost savings. Another desirable factor was that the costs in Britain were 60% less than that in Germany which would allow BMW to significantly reduce their costs. Finally, Rover already had successful products in markets that BMW did not have a current presence in but wanted to enter.

The initial terms of this acquisition sounds like it would be a success but, in fact, it was a failure. One major barrier was the ability to communicate. The language barrier between middle managers and engineers for both companies was significant so it was very difficult to complete activities effectively and efficiently. Also, lack of communication and coordination caused the strategic plan to get stuck at top level management where it did not successfully trickle down to all employees.

This case gives a great example of completing full due diligence and strategic planning. It is imperative that implementation is planned out clearly and closely controlled.

Chapter 8

Execution of Strategy

Executing strategies will result in failure if planning is not thorough and adequate. Several things should be considered to have an effective strategy implementation. These factors should be examined before an alternative is selected and then reviewed after strategy has been formulated. The purpose of the writing that follows is to detail some of those considerations that should be made.

Structure of Organization

Work is coordinated in an organization in a formal manner and that structure is referred to as organizational structure. An organization's highest purpose is to define a reporting structure for employees and dictating how work will be accomplished. It also shows what roles have decision making rights. There is not a "one size fits all" in organizational structures. Each organization may require a different type of structure. This portion of the chapter will help you understand the primary organization types and their impacts on strategic implementations.

As managers make strategic decisions, they should consult their organization structure to ensure that the strategies they consider and choose will fit with how the organization works. Organizational structures are not easily changed so choose strategies that fit closely to the structure if ideal. However, structures should be nimble enough to make some changes should a strategy require it. Ultimately, if you are starting from the beginning and developing your organization, your structure should be built around your strategy to make sure the strategies are effective.

In small startup companies, you often see an organizational structure of a few employees and an owner or manager. With this small number of employees, a formal structure is not required or even needed because each employee performs various different tasks and the owner/manager is generally involved in all aspects. This structure is called a simple structure. Depending on the business, this structure may change as the organization grows or stay the same because it will always be a small business. Since the owner/manager is involved with everything, they tend to communicate all strategic plans to the employees themselves on a regular basis.

As an organization grows, a need becomes apparent for a formal reporting structure and a hierarchy. This structure also gives organization to how and where work will be performed. Will it be performed by product team, function, or geographical locations?

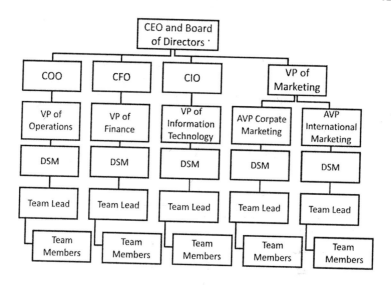

Vertical Growth

Vertical growth is defined as an increase in the length of an organization or an increase in the levels of an organization. The manager's span of control consists of the number of employees that report to that manager. A tall hierarchical organization has many levels but a small span of control. A flat organization has less levels and wider spans of control. Most organizations find their own happy medium between the two but in general can be referred to as mostly tall or mostly flat.

When a structure has been centralized, it means that the decisions are made at the top level of management due to an assumption that managers at these levels have greater experience and expertise. In this structure, decision making is slow because top level managers are not as knowledgeable as middle level and low-level managers. There is less buy in to these decisions as well since there was little involvement from them. The upside to this structure is that you often see more effective coordination and communication of the organization's mission, vision, and values to every employee. Planning and implementation are easily done as well because all employees are already involved.

Decentralized structures are just the opposite of centralized. Decisions are made by the lower level managers who have more knowledge of operations. Doing this allows organizations to take advantage of their knowledge capital and make better informed strategic decisions. For organizations whose focus is on customer service, decentralization is key because the low-level managers are closer to customers and their needs. The downside to decentralization is that the lines of accountability are blurred. The extent to which organizations are decentralized varies from organization to organization. Considerations like organization size, unrelated businesses and dynamic environments should be examined when deciding the extent of decentralization. In this structure, administrative costs are lower because there are fewer levels. Managers have more authority which increases their satisfaction and motivation. Innovation is also indirectly encouraged with the wider spectrum of freedom.

Horizontal Growth

In horizontal growth, the organization's structure expands. Employees can be involved with multiple activities, but one employee cannot be involved with all the activities in the organization. Expansion allows for development of more dedicated functions. As the size increases, so does the bureaucracy. Larger companies can be more efficient if managed adequately, but the opposite also holds true if managed poorly. Using a horizontal structure, organizations utilize less hierarchy levels and therefore reduces the bureaucratic issues.

Alternative Structural Forms

The following reading discusses different alternatives to horizontal and vertical growth.

Functional

People with similar tasks or responsibilities are assembled into a functional structure. This structure is one of the more common in organizations and it fosters quick decision making because the decision makers are easily able to communicate with one another. It can also address cost and quality issues effectively simply by grouping together functional areas. Another advantage is that people can learn new things from each other because they have similar skill sets and interests. A disadvantage of this structure is that functional groups may create silos and not communicate outside of their functional group which can affect creativity and innovation. It also reduces the accountability for profits and losses since they are organized around functions instead of regions or products. This structure is a fairly effective way of managing, controlling, and coordinating activities. It is probably most effective for those organizations defending their position in the market or low-cost organizations that focus on efficiencies. An example of a functional structure has been detailed below.

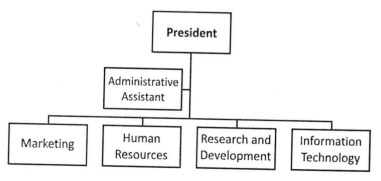

Divisional

Some organizations can outgrow the functional structure as they grow. When this happens, they look at implementing a multidivisional or a product divisional structure. A work team is created to foster inter-group relationships in order to meet the needs of the customer in a divisional structure. This structure allows for better production of varieties of similar products. Divisional structure is desirable because issues in one division do not directly affect the other divisions. In this structure, product lines are emphasized which results in better customer service. Responsibility for profits and losses are much more easily identified for accountability.

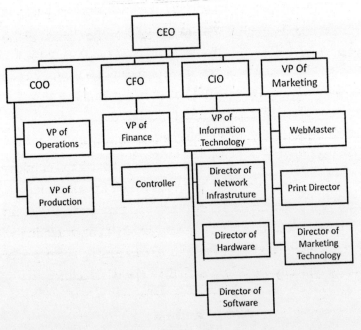

This is ideal for training team members, especially managers or other leaders. These employees can spend time in a specific product area and get in depth knowledge. Separating out into specialized functions can result in operational inefficiencies which is a disadvantage of this structure. There are typically multiple departments completing the same functions which can result in higher costs for human resources. Coordinating activities becomes more difficult and consistency is a challenge to achieve. Managers also tend to compete for the same resources instead of working together to a common goal. This structure works well with diversified organizational strategies.

Geographic Divisional

Divisions that are set up geographically, grouping employees into regions to work with each other producing similar products for a specific region is a geographic divisional structure. This can be used on a local basis, national basis or international basis. In this structure, products and services can cater to the climate of the region considering social, legal, and cultural aspects. Also producing or shipping products from different locations can provide a competitive advantage. For example, producing in countries where the supply or labor costs are low can provide a cost advantage. The disadvantages for this structure are very similar to product differential in that more functional employees are needed since every region needs its own functional teams. Coordination of activities is difficult, and managers tend to favor their own regions over working together in an organization-wide effort. Differentiated organizations or those using a prospector strategy typically work best with this type of structure.

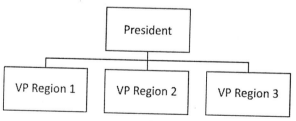

Matrix

One of the more complex structures it the matrix structure. It is complex because it groups people in two ways, by role performed and by the product group they work with. This structure gives team members more responsibility and ability to work independently. A benefit of this structure is increased productivity of the team, increased inventiveness, and ability to make decisions through group collaboration. This structure also creates complexity in chain of command and possible conflicts with employees and where their loyalties lie. Organizations concerned with cost leadership would not benefit from this structure. It is most commonly seen in industries that have a high rate of change such as the technology industry. You may see a matrix structure when special projects are being implemented in an organization.

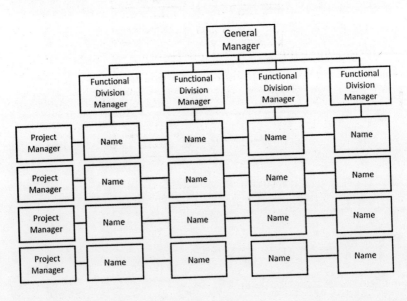

Evaluating Organizational Structure

In some organizations, it is easy to distinguish which structure they are using. Other companies use a mixture of all of the different structures to tailor a design for their organization. There are several popular organizations today that combine at least two if not more of the structures to meet the needs of the organization and its strategies. An example of what this might look like is below.

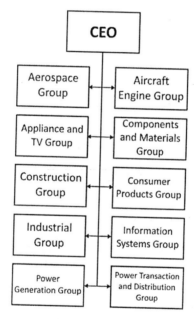

When attempting to determine which structure is best for your organization, be sure to consider the following:

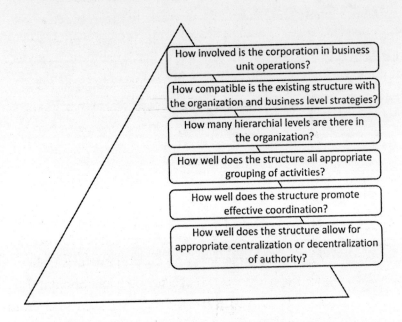

How involved is the corporation in business unit operations?

How compatible is the existing structure with the organization and business level strategies?

How many hierarchial levels are there in the organization?

How well does the structure all appropriate grouping of activities?

How well does the structure promote effective coordination?

How well does the structure allow for appropriate centralization or decentralization of authority?

Corporate Involvement in Operations

The level to which management is involved in operations varies from organization to organization. Sometimes this involvement is seen as a support for business units and other times, managers consider this a form of micromanaging. The level of corporate involvement can impact business profitability. For example, some organizations operate in a decentralized method with their unrelated businesses. In this manner, organizations have small corporate staffs and they empower business unit managers to do strategic and operation planning. On the opposite side, organizations that have units that are in the same industry or similar industries typically use centralization where big decisions are made at the corporate level.

Functional structures often give organizations the benefit of centralization. Since functional activities occur across a variety of business units, it is typically easier to make decisions at the corporate level. If you were to fast forward to the future in a centralized organization, you would see that it can also become inefficient because the organization is trying to tightly govern the activities being completed. As the organization grows, teams become larger and the distance between top level management and the employee grows. There is a greater dependence upon managers to trickle down communication to their staff. This process is full of communication and coordination problems as well as bureaucracy.

At this point, decentralization is the alternative organizations look at to address these issues. Many organizations that are focused on decentralization look at implementing a matrix structure. Doing this allows knowledge experts to make key decisions about the products and services they are involved in. Product divisional and geographic divisional structures will usually fall into either the functional or matrix category. There is a correlation between structure and levels of hierarchy in centralization and decentralization, but any structure can be used pursue either greater centralization or greater decentralization.

Restructuring Corporately

When organizations are performing poorly, they often consider a major restructure. The goal of this restructure is to improve efficiencies and performance. Sometimes these can be simple changes but more often than not, they are radical changes completed in the hopes of giving the organization a boost. Organizations that want to stay current choose to use corporate restructuring before organizational decline rather than at the time of decline. It is worth noting that organizations that do not plan for value may be forced to restructure by another organization which can be costly.

When completed appropriately, corporate restructuring can help a firm to implement its strategies more effectively. Changes to structure does have its downfalls. Restructuring does include activities such as closing offices, combining or eliminating positions. Organizations' human resource department must be involved in this process to avoid any conflict and help keep the focus on the competitive advantage. If not careful, job cuts damage morale, encourage employees to leave and discourages creativity because there is a focus on cutting costs.

Executing Strategic Change

Instituting strategic change can be a daunting challenge. The following sections will talk about two critical areas related to executing strategic change include organizational culture and leadership. Both of these should be oriented with strategy and controlled if the implementation of the strategy is to be effective.

Organizational Culture

Organizational culture is similar to the definition of culture. The only difference is that it is related to an organization. So, organizational culture means that a group of individuals who work for an organization share values and beliefs that dictate how they behave. This culture can be demonstrated in how an individual works, dresses, and performs on a daily basis. An organization's culture can either help or hinder its strategic actions. When cultures do not align with strategies, organizations generally do not perform as well as other organizations where their cultures and strategies are aligned. When the strategy and culture do not align, changing either one or both is a requirement. Changing culture is generally considered not as easy as changing strategy because changing culture requires substantial changes in expectations, standards, and ways of working.

Many organizations seek to achieve an adaptive culture where employees are willing to accept most change that is in alignment with the organization's core values. Such a culture is great for organizations that value innovation and high growth. Companies that are more conservative and unchanging, or inert cultures, are more invested in maintaining their existing resources. Google is a great example of a company where adaptive culture serves them well.

Changing Culture

Cultural change is a huge undertaking. Culture can be changed plans to do so often fail because there is lack of understanding of how to change culture and how long it takes. There are five ways that top management can impact and shape the organization's culture.

First, focus efforts on key areas of the organization. Measure and control the activities in those areas that are critical long-term performance and survival. Next, ensure the CEO is thoughtful of his responses to incidents and crises. His example of response can set the tone for other organization members. In this same vein, the CEO should consider himself a role model and act as he would want his associates to act. Others in the organization are likely to follow the CEO's lead. When you have determined desired behaviors and values, set up a reward system that gives incentives for associates to display those behaviors. Finally, stop recruiting for new associates "like you" and recruit associates that display the behaviors of the culture you wish to create.

Strategic Leadership

Top management sets the tone for the remaining managers and associates. When a strategic change is announced, organization members look to leaders to dictate their reactions and behaviors. To ensure successful change, the CEO and other management must model the behaviors they are looking for.

Every leader has a different style of leadership. This style consists of behaviors when managing and making decisions. Regardless of leadership style, whether inclusive or exclusive, it is in the leader's best interest to involve employees because this will improve their buy in and commitment.

There are two approaches to leadership style that relate leadership and strategy. The diagram below describes those approaches.

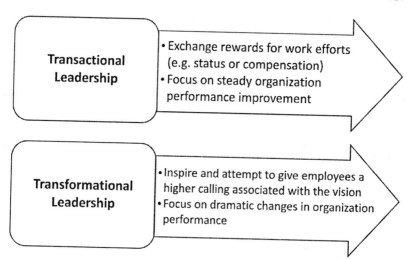

Typically, transformational leadership is related with strategies that focus on innovation. Steve Jobs was an excellent transformational leader who inspired his team members to go above and beyond their normal job responsibilities.

Transformational leadership also happens through a process that Austrian economist Joseph Schumpeter calls creative destruction. He describes this a way that managers break down old ways of doing things by building them back up with new and desired behavioral elements.

Most leaders have qualities that are typical to transactional and transformational leaders. Organizations tend to look for leaders who have styles that mesh well with the organization.

Implementing Change

Remember, top leadership and key managers must understand the need for change. This can prove challenging is the organization is currently performing well. Leadership must understand that the best plan is to be proactive and not reactive with strategy so making changing while you are performing well is the best time.

In summary, when an organization decides to implement a strategic change, they need to make sure to complete the following steps after they have thoroughly completed their analysis and strategy formulation.

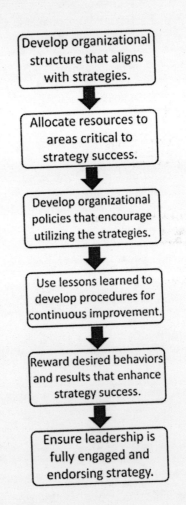